permission
to ponder

permission to ponder

CONTEMPLATIVE WISDOM FOR THE SPIRITUALLY DISTRACTED

Tracy Balzer

LEAFWOOD

PUBLISHERS

an imprint of Abilene Christian University Press

PERMISSION TO PONDER
Contemplative Wisdom for the Spiritually Distracted

LEAFWOOD
P U B L I S H E R S
an imprint of Abilene Christian University Press

Cover design by Thinkpen Design, LLC
Interior text design by Sandy Armstrong, Strong Design

Leafwood Publishers is an imprint of Abilene Christian University Press
ACU Box 29138
Abilene, Texas 79699

1-877-816-4455
www.leafwoodpublishers.com

15 16 17 18 19 20 / 7 6 5 4 3 2 1

For Margaret Therkelsen—
lover of Jesus
spiritual director
contemplative

acknowledgments

It is foolish to write a book about prayer without some pray-ers to back you up. Kim, Becci, and Lisa, my *lectio divina* group, were that for me. Heartfelt thanks to them for their prayers as I wrote, and for their ongoing lives of prayer that speak more loudly than the words on these pages ever will.

I'm grateful for Lauren Winner's ongoing role as "book doula" in my life. It was Lauren who asked me, over ten years ago, "So when are you going to write a book?" And in the midst of writing my second book, she cheered for my idea of looking at life through a *lectio* lens. So here's that "baby" number three. Thank you, Lauren, for your willingness to share your wisdom with a neophyte writer like me.

Many thanks to Leonard Allen, now at Lipscomb University, for accepting the proposal for this book, and to my editor, Mary Hardegree, and the staff at Leafwood Publishers for their expertise and support.

The encouragement of my colleagues and friends at John Brown University and my students (who teach me daily) have fueled this writing, as have the prayers of a wide circle of friends around the country. I am likewise forever grateful for the spiritual home that Subiaco Abbey has become for me. The brothers there bless me with Benedictine hospitality and teach me about contemplation in action.

As always, my love and thanks are especially directed toward my family: Cary, Kelsey and Jordan, and Langley. Yes, they've been patient with me as I write, but I am most grateful for their patience as I struggle—and often fail—to be the prayerful wife, mom, and friend I want to be.

table of contents

foreword

It is hard to be a Christ-follower in a world that devalues discipleship, slowing down, silence, listening, prayer, and the attainment of contemplative wisdom. The value system of the world we live in centers on success, money, possessions, and achievements. As a result, few people have the courage to pursue the deeper life. In his landmark 1987 book, *Celebration of Discipline*, Richard J. Foster opens with this provocative line: "Superficiality is the curse of our age." Nearly thirty years later, his observation remains true—but the conditions have seemingly worsened. In 1987, we had no cell phones, no Internet, and, thus, none of the time-killing, attention-distracting websites and apps that plague us today. I once heard the comedian Dennis Miller say that the attention span of the average person in America is like that of "a ferret on a triple espresso."

We are distracted and exhausted, and, ironically, we are bored. In our boredom we seek escape, and we are offered it in increasing measure and speed. We live in the Information Age. I have access to more information on my smart phone than exists in the Harvard Library. We have more information, but, typically, less wisdom. Tracy Balzer begins this fine book with a poem by T. S. Eliot, wherein the writer laments, "Where is the Life we have lost in living? Where is wisdom we have lost in knowledge? Where is the knowledge we have lost in *information*?" (italics mine). We live in the Information Age, but we have lost knowledge and wisdom, and are no longer Living.

Superficiality is epidemic in the current age of information and entertainment. Superficiality is the curse of our age, and *hurry-sickness* is the number one illness of our age. Pressed with too much to do and too little time, hurry becomes our modus operandi. Nearly everyone I know, when asked how things are going, will say, "I am just so busy." If someone responded, "I am well, I am rested, I am enjoying margin in my life, and I am experiencing deep contentment in my life with God," we might think something was seriously wrong with her, or at the very least, that she was lazy. And yet, if someone did say that, something is seriously right with her, and seriously wrong with the rest of us who know only exhaustion and inattention.

Hurry-sickness is deadly to our souls. You cannot do anything important in the spiritual life in a hurry. You cannot pray in a hurry. You cannot love in a hurry. You cannot listen in a hurry. Hurry—and its sister, worry—shrivel the soul. The soul needs space and silence, gratitude and blessing, contemplation and rest, prayer and worship. Yet everything about our culture is pushing us away from what matters the most: the cure and care of our souls, and learning to live wisely and well. That is why this book is important for us today. This book tells the story of one person's effort to step out of the swift current of modern culture in order to step into the slow and still presence of beauty, goodness, and truth. In other words, to connect with God.

We are driven to hurriedness and distraction because of the false narrative that pervades modern culture, summed up in this idea: "My value is determined by my accomplishments." It has other slogans as well: "I am what I do." In our search for significance, we swallow this bait, and end up in a frantic, frenetic, and fruitless pursuit to achieve, to do, and to become. We become human *do*-ings, not human beings. Thus, we end up living superficial lives, endlessly concerned with trying to get others—and even ourselves—to think well of us. No more do we pursue depth and wisdom. Our culture tells us we have little need for them.

In this book, Tracy is on a search for wisdom. She calls it *contemplative* wisdom, because she knows that one cannot be wise without being contemplative. Dallas Willard defines wisdom as "knowledge of how to live well." Tracy is longing to live well. You sense her passion on every page. This is perhaps my favorite thing about Tracy, and about this book. She is on a search for depth. St. Augustine was on a similar search for depth, which led him to peer into his inner depths. He was stunned by how much was beneath the surface, how massive his own soul was: countless memories, a vast imagination, powerful and rich feelings and emotions. The inner depth, he discovered, was endless, and this fact led him to God, a God he said was closer to us than we are to ourselves.

While the world distracts and discounts the pursuit of contemplative wisdom, this book offers hope. Hope is badly needed today. Where does hope come from? Hope is essentially faith in a good future, based on the past and present. Faith is an extension of knowledge. I come to know God's faithfulness, and thus am able, based on that knowledge, to exercise it in the present moment by trusting God. Hope is my posture of faith toward the future. But it is based on what God has done and is doing. Thus, a book like this brings me hope because I see how God was faithful to Tracy. He showed up for her, he blessed her in this pursuit, and thus, he can show up for me, and he can show up for you. Faith and hope are best summed up in the words of Julian of Norwich, who plays a part in this book. She said, "All is well, and all is well, and all manner of things shall be well."

This book will give you a glimpse not merely of *lectio divina* (though it is a central practice) but also of a *vida divina* (a divine life), or as Tracy puts it, a "*lectio* for life." I was struck by her passionate question in Chapter Thirteen: "How can I live daily in the reality of Jesus' embrace?" That is at the core of this book. It is not a how-to on being still, or going on a pilgrimage, or paying better attention, though it includes all of that. It is a journey into the embrace of God, one that can be felt only when we slow down and turn to God. May that good and beautiful God Tracy encountered, encounter you as you read.

James Bryan Smith

introduction

The endless cycle of idea and action,
Endless invention, endless experiment,
Brings knowledge of motion, but not of stillness;
Knowledge of speech, but not of silence;
Knowledge of words, and ignorance of the Word.
All our knowledge brings us nearer to our ignorance,
All our ignorance brings us nearer to death,
But nearness to death no nearer to God.
Where is the Life we have lost in living?
Where is the wisdom we have lost in knowledge?
Where is the knowledge we have lost in information?
The cycles of Heaven in twenty centuries
Bring us farther from God and nearer to the Dust.

—T. S. Eliot, *The Rock*[1]

As a young woman struggling to raise my children well, to be an encouraging and helpful partner to my husband, to be a good friend to a few and of meaningful service to a few more, I often found myself looking forward to the day when I possessed something like wisdom. I recall sitting in the audience at a writer's conference, listening with admiration as Madeleine L'Engle described herself as a WOW—a Wise Old Woman. I wondered how long it would take for me to be able to describe myself that way. Thirty years later, I'm still asking that question.

I suppose I have collected a few bits of wisdom along the way, some of which are less important than others. For example, always take your passport out of your jeans pocket before washing them. (Yes, I have a story.) Also, buying tomatoes in the grocery store is generally pointless. Next, the book is almost always better than the movie (read the book first). And my most valuable bit of wisdom thus far: multi-tasking is highly overrated. This is a bit of a blow, because multitasking is something I happen to be pretty good at. I can make plane reservations while answering a text while checking my email with the best of them. It's completely stressful, but I can do it. The world seems to highly regard such skills, so the good news is that I will probably remain employed.

But in the core of my being, I know that I am more than what I do. Despite what the rest of the world says, whether it's an employer, or a family member, or that very loud voice inside my own head, multitasking and being superproductive only goes so far. This is particularly relevant when considering the spiritual realm, the landscape of the soul. All of that "doing" in our lives can only possibly make sense if it emerges from a place of inner health and peace.

For the Christian, for me, that requires focused attention to God—to his Word and to his activity in the world. Multitasking has no real place when it comes to living life with Jesus. He showed us as much, making a determined escape when the crowds began pressing in with all their expectations of who he should be.

The distractions of the world too easily pull me away, crowding out his voice and dulling the effects of the transforming work he wants to do in me. When I cave in to the many distractions of life on this earth and ignore the deeper, inner work that the Spirit of God is concerned about, the result is that superficial living becomes the rule of the day. And spiritually superficial people don't tend to make lasting contributions anyway.

"Superficial living." I don't know about you, but that phrase leaves sort of a bile-flavored residue in my heart and mind. Living a superficial life isn't a sin; it just isn't very interesting, and it has a very temporal feel to it. It feels wasteful. Life is too short to merely live on the surface of things. And for the Christian who believes Jesus when he said that he would give us an abundant life, we know that he wasn't talking about stuff or status; there is more to life than what we can see. We know that life lived on a spiritual plane should be marked by things like mercy and forgiveness and love—all of which begin inwardly, in an invisible place, and work themselves out in the physical realm. Christians know that we are empowered by an invisible God, specifically the Holy Spirit, who works his transforming power inwardly in us to bring about external change—change in us and change in the world. This is what we call spiritual formation.

With that in mind, then, those who follow Jesus cannot afford to live superficial lives. We need to give attention to the internal state of our souls so that we can be fully engaged in the work God has for us to do. But sadly, most of us dive headlong into the work first, giving only cursory attention to our own spiritual health. We are very busy and effective ministers and teachers and parents and community members ... but our human reserves last only so long. Superficial living eventually loses its ability to satisfy us, but more importantly, our effectiveness in the world is limited by it. There's only so much that can be done when we remain on the surface, because our own spiritual transformation is stunted.

Here's a way to think about it: I love the ocean but, sadly, am not a great swimmer. Seriously. Thanks to a sinus surgery in my late teens, I lack the ability to keep water from rushing up my nose and down my throat, which makes doing anything underwater a real challenge. I need some help if I'm going to discover and enjoy what's going on underneath the surface of the ocean. So I rent some basic equipment—a snorkel and some fins—that I learn to use properly, and soon enough I am seeing amazing things that are other-wise beyond my ability to experience: yellow tang, threadfin butterflyfish, brightly colored coral. If you've done this, you know the sensation of suddenly becoming part of a great saltwater aquarium. For someone like me, who is otherwise unable to go underwater, it's a phenomenal experience. I'm doing something that I cannot otherwise do on my own.

But what if I want to see and experience the things that lurk more than fifteen feet below the surface? I need to get different equipment and different skills: scuba gear and training. I need to wear the proper clothes—a wetsuit—and I need an oxygen tank, since breathing on my own at those depths is not an option, not just for me but for any human. After being trained and changed into something that functions more effectively in the deep, I can (so I've heard) experience the reality of undersea life: sea turtles, rays, maybe an octopus. Are you getting the idea?

What if I get really serious about ocean exploration and want to go even deeper? What if I'm convinced that fantastic discoveries are waiting for me, that I'm hungry for more of what goes on down there, and that maybe the things I discover there are so great I want to share them with folks on the shore? Well, then I clearly need much more sophisticated equipment, some sort of ocean-floor vehicle that completely changes me, so to speak, into something that can thrive and function well in that alien environment. There's some healthy trepidation involved, going deep like that. But one thing is for sure, the deeper I want to go, the more I have to change.

And what incredible discoveries await those who are willing to go through the process.

A Vision for What Matters

The Apostle Paul addressed the church at Corinth, trying to explain to them the difference between the wisdom of the world and the wisdom that comes from God. He said even the wisdom that comes from God is something of a mystery; it cannot be discerned or discovered without the assistance of the Holy Spirit.

> "What no eye has seen,
>   what no ear has heard,
> and what no human mind has conceived"—
>   the things God has prepared for those
>   who love him—
>   these are the things God has revealed to us by
>   his Spirit.

The Spirit searches all things, even the deep things of God. For who knows a person's thoughts except their own spirit within them? In the same way no one knows the thoughts of God except the Spirit of God. What we have received is not the spirit of the world, but the Spirit who is from God, so that we may understand what God has freely given us. This is what we speak, not in words taught us by human wisdom but in words taught by the Spirit, explaining spiritual realities with Spirit-taught words. *The person without the Spirit does not accept the things that come from the Spirit of God but considers them foolishness, and cannot*

> *understand them because they are discerned only through*
> *the Spirit.* (1 Cor. 2:9–14; italics mine)

In the same way that oceanography requires submitting to the laws of the sea, the deep things of God require submission to the laws of the Spirit. The discoveries of the depths are simply not available to those who are driven by the distractions of surface living.

To enter into the deeper things of God, we must recognize that the satisfaction of surface living is short-lived and that we have to willfully engage in God's desire for our transformation. It will take a lifetime of submission to the training and equipment the Holy Spirit has for us. But the treasures that await us—stillness of soul, a grateful humility, deep reverence for God in his holiness, and a clearer vision of Jesus—are just some of the richly rewarding changes that come into our lives when we turn away from the superficiality of life and enter into the deep, deep love of Jesus.

The world you live in does not think this is a good idea. You may not even think it's possible. But Jesus himself is giving you permission, permission to ponder deeply who he is. The ancients called this *contemplation*.

In a curious way, the concept of contemplation was hovering over me long before I could recognize it or had a name for it. "In its most basic and fundamental expression, Contemplative Prayer is a loving attentiveness to God."[2] As a young adult, I was a thoroughgoing evangelical Protestant, a graduate of a Christian liberal arts university. I'd been trained in discipleship and was a good reader of the current popular Christian material. I had led small groups and Bible studies. I had access to plenty of information and good answers for anyone who challenged my Christian faith. But there was a section of my soul that remained hungry.

That's when I met Margaret, a tall, wise Kentucky woman whose contemplative passion ran deep. She consented to become my spiritual director and convinced me that "Honey, nothing satisfies like Jesus."

Years later, as a young mother of two and a busy pastor's wife, I struggled to understand how a life with so many demands could coalesce with that kind of intimacy with God. I was confronted with the difficulties that all modern people of faith face: distractions. Wanting to go deeper with God was one thing; doing it was another. Happy as I was with my position in life, it did become clear to me that my world was full of distractions, leaving precious little room for prayers or thoughts that took longer than five minutes. And this was all before the Internet, before email, and before Facebook was a twinkle in Mark Zuckerberg's eye.

In the midst of the fray, I got wind of an opportunity that offered hope for addressing my dilemma: one of my favorite authors and teachers would be leading a silent retreat at a now-defunct women's monastery in Vancouver, British Columbia. She would teach a small group of Christians how to listen to God in silence. I had taken a journaling class from her a year before, and I trusted her with spiritual matters (she was most definitely a WOW). I also trusted the inner tug of the Holy Spirit that told me this might help me sort out my spiritual dilemma.

The retreat was a three-hour drive from my home in Seattle up to British Columbia. From the get-go, God made it clear to me just exactly what would be necessary if I hoped to address my inner frustrations: I needed to reintegrate my fragmented life. I needed to cease striving. I needed to make some changes so I could go deeper with God, to get away from surface living.

The retreat center in Vancouver proved to be an ideal setting for people like me who needed to step away from their active lives to be still. We were given excellent instruction on how to effectively traverse the distance between noise and silence. There was a walking trail on the property, densely populated with the green and flowering vegetation that is so typical of the Pacific Northwest. Our private rooms, simple as they were, helped quiet our fidgety minds. There were art supplies and books in the common room for our use and perusal. And our leader validated our need for a short nap, for after all, God "grants sleep to those he loves" (Ps. 127:2).

Mealtimes were spent together; some were open for discussion, and others called for silence. A few of the silent meals were accompanied by a single voice reading from Scripture or a spiritually enriching book, keeping us in step with the monastic tradition. And there were scheduled times together in the afternoon and evening when we shared our responses to practices that we had been assigned throughout the day.

I look back on that silent retreat as a spiritual marker in my life. At that retreat, I identified a part of myself that was known, but unnamed. I remember talking with fellow retreatants, otherwise unknown to me, yet as familiar as if we had grown up together. They spoke about prayer and God in ways that struck a strong and harmonious chord; it was like discovering an entire family that talked together like good families should. I felt like I had found "my people" and soaked up the enriching conversations, the shared passion for Christ and his presence, and the belief that the life of faith had to be more than just running around like crazy all the time.

I learned that there is hope for the spiritually distracted soul—for people like me, whose lives were full of many good things, but whose souls seemed to be atrophying even in the midst of those many good things. What I learned was that an overly busy soul is a distracted soul, and a distracted soul will find it increasingly impossible to know the deep things of God.

The Invitation

Come, all you who are thirsty,
come to the waters;
and you who have no money,
come, buy and eat!
Come, buy wine and milk

> without money and without cost.
> Why spend money on what is not bread,
>   and your labor on what does not satisfy?
> Listen, listen to me, and eat what is good,
>   and you will delight in the richest of fare.
> Give ear and come to me;
>   listen, that you may live.
>
> (Isa. 55:1-5)

Is there a sweeter invitation? The manner in which the prophet Isaiah communicates God's graciousness and generosity here is at once tender and indisputable. This is an invitation from the one who knows exactly what we need to thrive: his words are food and drink and are free to any who hunger and thirst. It's an invitation that has been accessible for millennia by the people of God, and yet we carry on working for and buying nourishment of our own liking, turning a blind eye to what God has offered. We settle for the apple when we've had access to an entire Garden.

We are happy enough with the easy-access choice. Sound and media and people are default excuses for ignoring the state of our souls. Plunging headfirst into a pool full of classes to teach, emails to write, and students to counsel is disturbingly natural for me, whereas silence and stillness before God is as otherworldly as swimming in the depths of the sea. Doing nothing, just being with God, is impossible when the voice in my head condemns me for squandering time that could be spent checking things off a list somewhere. Yes, I want God desperately. But that doesn't mean I don't, even after all these years, still choose poorly.

The Need for Reflection

Rushing cancels reflection. Pausing to attune our whole being in awe and wonder to the mystery that embraces us enhances the efficacy of our apostolate. It prevents us from placing ourselves at the center of reality instead of the Divine Forming Mystery. Contemplative presence draws us in peace and silence to new disclosures of our destiny as friends and servants of God. Frantic as functionalism may make us, it cannot disturb our encounters with Christ, who invites us to come away and be with him a while.[3]

It's distressing how few Christian churches assist us in this dilemma. When was the last time you were given more than sixty seconds to pray in a service, or given space to ponder the Scripture that has been read (if it indeed has been read)? Why do we feel that our worship services must mirror the pace of our everyday lives? Shouldn't it be the opposite? Shouldn't the church be at least one place where space for God is in abundance?

I remember my first experience in a liturgical church. Where many evangelicals might find elements of the service distracting—the complex liturgy, standing and kneeling, crossing oneself and prewritten prayers—I came to the end of the service with a profound realization: *I just thought about*

God for an entire hour. For me, there had been precious few distractions. In fact, the service and the church itself seemed to work overtime to get me to focus. I listened to extended passages of the Word of God, rather than quietly critiquing the pastor's sermon. I digested the prayer of confession, rather than puzzling over the new worship song. The Spirit of God was giving me the equipment I needed to leave the surface and take a deeper dive.

In her book *Quiet: The Power of Introverts in a World That Can't Stop Talking,* Susan Cain makes some observations about modern evangelical churches that contribute to our battle with distractions. "If you don't love Jesus out loud, then it must not be real love."[4] I don't know Cain's personal perspective on faith, or if she has faith at all. But her point is an interesting one: if our worship services are so full of noise and speaking and performing, when does God get a chance to speak?

> Oh, the depth of the riches of the wisdom and
>   knowledge of God!
>   How unsearchable his judgments,
>   and his paths beyond tracing out! (Rom. 11:33)

This book is an effort to learn how others have accepted the invitation from God to dwell deeply, to drink up the nourishing presence of Christ in our midst, beginning with faithful followers of Jesus in the Gospels. Specifically, we will enter into episodes in the lives of biblical women I am calling "The Four Marys." You will see soon enough that there are actually only three women—Mary of Bethany, Mary the mother of Jesus, and Mary Magdalene—but we will visit one of them twice.

I have spent a lot of time with these Marys, and they are teaching me, by example, what it means to live a life of full attention to Jesus. These are not multitasking women. These are not women who were willing to live on the surface; they insisted on going deep with Jesus. While the disciples panicked over storms and squabbled over who would be first in the kingdom, the Marys each chose an alternate approach—one chose to listen, one pondered in humility, one reverently adored, and one learned how to truly see.

This book, therefore, is basically divided into four sections, each led by one of the Marys. Through each story, we will witness the contemplative characteristics of the believer who effectively manages the distractions of life in order to give loving attention to what is most important. God himself gives us permission to contemplate, to meditate, and to ponder the whole spectrum of miraculous evidence of God's presence among us through Word, sacrament, and creation.

Can we give that same permission to ourselves?

Notes

[1] T. S. Eliot, *The Complete Poems and Plays, 1909–1950* (Orlando, FL: Harcourt Brace, 1980), 96.

[2] Richard Foster, *Prayer: Finding the Heart's True Home* (New York: HarperCollins, 1992), 158.

[3] Susan Muto, "Living Contemplatively and Serving God in the World," *Journal of Spiritual Formation and Soul Care* 6, no. 1 (2013): 91.

[4] Susan Cain, *Quiet: The Power of Introverts in a World That Can't Stop Talking* (New York: Crown, 2012), 67.

contemplation considered

In an age of acceleration, nothing can be more exhilarating than going slow. And in an age of distraction, nothing is so luxurious as paying attention. And in an age of constant movement, nothing is so urgent as sitting still.

—Pico Ayer[1]

For those of us who wrestle with the frustration of distractions—things that draw us away from what is real and true and invisible and move us toward the things that are superficial and transitory—the psalm writer has a bit of coaching for us. I return to the following psalm over and over, because in the midst of a distracted life, I am once again presented with a clear image of what life is all about, the kind of life that I am to be pursuing.

> Blessed is the one
> who does not walk in step with the wicked

> or stand in the way that sinners take
>> or sit in the company of mockers,
> but whose delight is in the law of the LORD,
>> and who meditates on his law day and night.
> That person is like a tree planted by streams of water,
>> which yields its fruit in season
> and whose leaf does not wither—
>> whatever they do prospers.
>
> (Ps. 1:1–3)

The psalm writer sets out to teach us what such a life is like, using a healthy, thriving tree as an example. If I want this God-focused, undistracted life, then like a tree, I am to be planted. That word "planted" brings the image of a farmer sowing seed and makes me think about the beginnings of living things. We plant seeds in hopes that something will grow. But the word "planted" also indicates permanence, stability, immovability. Yes, a tree grows because it has been planted; it grows strong and mature because it remains planted.

Years ago, my husband and young daughter rescued a sapling that was off to a good start on the edge of the woods across the road from our house. The adolescent tree stood right in the path of certain doom because city workers periodically clear the sides of our road to create some semblance of a shoulder. Cary, my husband, and Kelsey, around twelve at the time, felt it their moral duty to step in and give the tree a chance for a longer life. So, one afternoon, they took their shovels across the road and endeavored to transplant it. Now, a decade, a college degree, and a marriage later, Kelsey boasts that their efforts were not in vain. The thing is huge, a great sprawling sycamore. Not only was it planted on that day years ago, it remains planted, immovable, with branches towering above the roofline of our house.

That tree has claimed its spot in our yard, and it gives me a start when I encounter the bumpy evidence of its root system many feet away from its trunk. If we ever need to move this tree, it will take much more than a dad and a girl and two shovels. What a contrast my sycamore is to the distracted lives we live. Where it is firmly planted and immovable, we flit about, chasing after every external attraction and demand, oblivious to the voice that says, "Be still."

The psalm writer also says that this tree thrives because it is planted by "streams of water." It is a lovely, pastoral scene, to be sure, and we have no doubt that trees should have access to a water source. This is basic, third grade biology. Why does the psalm writer feel the need to be so painfully obvious? Perhaps he knows that, unlike trees, we humans can actually choose our water source. As beings who have been given the gift of free will by our Creator, we can decide the manner in which our souls will be watered.

So it's not only necessary for me to be planted—to be firm and immovable in my desire to be with God always—but to make the choice to be properly nourished. I wonder, sometimes, if our tendency to blame distractions for our spiritual fickleness is just a way of disguising what is really going on. Sometimes we simply choose something other than the better way. Instead of the clear, chemical-free water that flows from the heart of God, we drink from sources that are tainted, brackish, hardened by additives. In our frantic lives, it is indeed tempting to adopt a diet of the easy spirituality touted by celebrities or best-selling authors, especially because it seems to carry us along just fine. When you are in survival mode, hanging on for dear life to anything that can get you through, the imitation of what is true and clean and clear has to be good enough.

Yet we know that kind of life is ultimately disappointing, unsatisfying, and definitely not nourishing. Such a tree will not "bear fruit in season." You know this to be true personally, and I'm guessing that is why you are reading this book. If you want to thrive, says the psalm writer, you must be planted and you must drink deeply of the water of God. And just in case we're not getting it, he makes his point painfully clear: such a person delights in the law of the Lord *and meditates on his law day and night.*

This is the prescription for us, plain but not altogether simple. The distractions in life are real, and they will not stop as long as our brains are capable of noticing them. What we must be convinced of is that reflection and meditation are legitimate elements of the God-loving life. Yes, there is much to be done in this world, and we are the redemptive agents who are called to duty. But in the same way that a tree cannot bear fruit unless it is planted by a dependable water source, we cannot fulfill our divine appointment as redemptive agents in this world with any substantial measure of effectiveness if we refuse to drink of the spiritual nutrients that meditation affords.

God is not impressed with all of our doing for doing's sake; on the contrary, God has given us full permission to dwell with him in such a way that a deep and soul-shaping love for him and love for others is the result.

Words and Their Meanings

Words like "meditation" and "contemplation" are loaded with meaning and laden with possibilities for misuse and misunderstanding. Because they have been attached to secular spiritualities and utilized by Eastern religions, we are often quick to dismiss them as anti-Christian practices. Entire websites and organizations have been established by Christians who are no doubt well-meaning, but who frankly reveal themselves to be overly fearful and lacking the kind of careful study and discipline that is required when thinking critically about such subjects.

Some are concerned that such practices may open us up to spiritually destructive forces, "[f]or our struggle is not against flesh and blood, but against the rulers, against the authorities, against the powers of this dark world and against the spiritual forces of evil in the heavenly realms" (Eph. 6:12). There is a fear that entering into deep prayer in stillness and relinquishment makes us especially vulnerable to forces of darkness. I do not want to minimize the role of the Enemy in this world, nor easily dismiss his intention to sideline Christians at every opportunity. But there is much more to Ephesians 6 than this single verse about powers of the dark world.

The greater context is the exhortation for believers to put on the full armor of God. We are given instructions on how to be ready and not fearful, resulting in a formidable soldier who is equipped "so that you can take your stand against the devil's schemes" (v. 11). In fact, the passage tells us to "pray in the Spirit on all occasions with all kinds of prayers and requests" (v. 18). Our ever-deepening prayer need not be accompanied by fear.

Other Christians are concerned by the practice of meditation and contemplation on the extreme liberal end of the theological spectrum, resulting in less of a Scripture-centered or Christ-centered practice, with all sorts of dubious objectives. To be sure, critical thinking is in order to guard against any practice or belief that does not have its root in Scripture and the tenets of orthodoxy.

With the clear intent to operate under the authoritative guidance of holy Scripture, and the confidence that the Spirit of God is greater than any evil intent on sidelining us, we can confidently proceed with a vision of a deeper connection with God before us.

Lectio Divina—Sacred Reading

Many modern evangelical Christians—perhaps you are one of them—have recovered the ancient practice of praying the Scriptures via the pattern of *lectio divina*.[2] For me, *lectio divina* has proven to be an enriching and effective spiritual practice, especially in light of my ongoing battle with distractions. And because it has been practiced by so many Christians for many centuries, I feel confident in practicing it, teaching it, recommending it. If it is new to you, a brief introduction will be helpful as we explore ways of escaping superficial spirituality and entering into the depths. Understanding *lectio* will prove helpful in our discussion.

Lectio divina has its root in Benedictine monasticism and is still today given a place of high honor in the life of modern monks. The earliest writing about *lectio* is from Guigo, a monk in the twelfth century, who wrote about a "ladder for monks by which they rise from earth to heaven,"[3] consisting of four prayer movements (the rungs of his ladder), each of which begins with the slow rereading of a short scripture: reading the passage (*lectio*), meditation on the passage (*meditatio*), prayer in response to the passage (*oratio*), and contemplation of the love of God (*contemplatio*). "Reading is listening to God's word, while meditation, prayer and contemplation are degrees of responding to his word. . . . The entire process becomes a means of going from the word of God back to God, a method of prayer. Listening to the text and then responding lead to an experience of God who is the ultimate speaker behind the particular message."[4]

For Christians who find prayer difficult in a world of distractions, *lectio divina* not only gives some structural support, it reminds us that prayer, in its purest form, does not rely on our initiative. Rather, prayer is, as Eugene Peterson often reminds us, always an answering response to God, who always has the first word. *Lectio divina* helps us listen to God first, and then prompts a response from us.

As a young undergraduate student at a Christian liberal arts university, my mind was fairly blown when I learned how to study the Scriptures—how to research historical context and original language, how to gain a fuller understanding via literary considerations like author and genre, how to come to the Scriptures inductively and objectively. These foundational skills are essential for any Christian as we seek to ascertain the truest, most accurate interpretation of the sacred text. Our pursuit of God and his ways must be undergirded with good theology, and good theology is rooted in good biblical exegesis.

But the living and active Word of God does not only speak to us at the intellectual level. It also speaks to us at the emotional, heart-and-soul level. We can come to the Bible for the purpose of meeting God, rather than simply gaining more information about him. We believe God is a Person, and by his Spirit he speaks to us, giving us wisdom, guidance, assurance, correction, compassion, mercy. We are changed not just in our minds, but in our hearts, and the changes work their way from the inside out so that more and more we resemble Christ. *Lectio divina* brings us to the feet of Jesus, and we feast on the Word as he feeds us, attending to the deepest needs of our souls. It bridges the gap between what Robert Mulholland describes as "reading for information" and "reading for transformation."[5]

The habit of listening during sacred reading fosters the attitude of listening in other situations to what the word of God is asking. . . . Fidelity to sacred reading should work a gradual change in the reader's relationships with other people, helping him or her become more generous, considerate, gentle, and less selfish, cranky, gossipy, touchy. Sacred reading spreads out into daily life as a power of ongoing reformation and conversation and enabling the reader to recognize and respond to the word of God spoken at diverse times and circumstances.[6]

The contemplative practice of *lectio divina* is a way of engaging with the Word so that God can use it to change us more into the image of his Son. "*Lectio* is meeting with a friend, a very special Friend who is God; listening to him, really listening; and responding, in intimate prayer and in the way we take that Word with us and let it shape our lives."[7]

Lectio Divina for Life

In recent years, I have discovered that the pattern of *lectio divina* with respect to Scripture has spilled out and over with respect to my life. As I read, ponder, submit, and rest in Scripture's fullness via *lectio divina*, it has become apparent that the same pattern is valuable as I endeavor to grasp God's truth and beauty in the everyday business of life in the world. This is helpful indeed, for as Christians who live in this time-between-times, in the already-but-not-yet of

God's kingdom, we are not to passively wait for eternity to enjoy God; his Spirit is alive and among us and in us now, on this earth. I am not just waiting to see him one day; I am looking for him in my life today.

If *lectio divina* has helped me focus and listen better to the Word of God on the page, perhaps it can teach me something about listening better to the Word of God as I go about my ordinary living. One of the great frustrations about being spiritually distracted is that we find ourselves living bifurcated lives. We segregate our lives into categories: spiritual, career, family, recreation. We talk about searching for balance as if each category needs to be equal in weight. Shouldn't we rather be thinking about how *each* of the pieces and parts of our lives are spiritual? Shouldn't we walk as disciples into every arena in which we find ourselves? Paul encouraged us to pray continually (1 Thess. 5:17), not simply because that's what "good Christians" do, but because life is best lived when we are continually mindful of the presence of God.

In the chapters ahead, we will see how the practice of *lectio divina* not only helps us prayerfully ponder Scripture, but how it can also help us prayerfully ponder *life*. The Four Marys will serve as our models and guides as we use *lectio, meditatio, oratio*, and *contemplatio* as lenses through which we will look at life.

Whether applied to the prayerful reading of Scripture or the prayerful reading of life, the most important aspect of contemplation is that its objective is always *love*. Richard

Foster says that the contemplative tradition is "a life of loving attention to God."[8] For all of the ways that the term "contemplation" is misused and misapplied, and for all of the various non-Christian contexts in which it is used, this definition of contemplation must, I believe, be our polestar. This commitment to loving God and receiving his love in return is what will keep us grounded in the Great Commandment and in the life of Jesus.

And isn't that what a distracted life most desperately needs?

Notes

[1] Pico Iyer, "The Art of Stillness," TEDSalon NY2014, filmed August 2014, https://www.ted.com/talks/pico_iyer_the_art_of_stillness?language=en.

[2] The pronunciation commonly used in sacred contexts is "lect-see-oh."

[3] Charles Cummings, *Monastic Practices* (Kalamazoo, MI: Cistercian, 1986), 15.

[4] Ibid.

[5] Robert Mulholland, *Invitation to a Journey* (Madison, WI: InterVarsity, 1993), 111.

[6] Cummings, *Monastic Practices*, 18.

[7] M. Basil Pennington, *Lectio Divina: Renewing the Ancient Practice of Praying the Scriptures* (New York: Crossroad, 1998), xi.

[8] Richard Foster, *Streams of Living Water: Celebrating the Great Traditions of Christian Faith* (New York: HarperCollins, 1998), 58.

the first mary: *lectio*

As Jesus and his disciples were on their way, he came to a village where a woman named Martha opened her home to him. She had a sister called Mary, who sat at the Lord's feet listening to what he said. But Martha was distracted by all the preparations that had to be made. She came to him and asked, "Lord, don't you care that my sister has left me to do the work by myself? Tell her to help me!"

"Martha, Martha," the Lord answered, "you are worried and upset about many things, but few things are needed—or indeed only one. Mary has chosen what is better, and it will not be taken away from her." (Luke 10:38–42)

The Mary-Martha story is the go-to narrative when discussing the value of *being* versus *doing*. Mary is rightly upheld as the one who chose the "better" part, and for years she has inflicted guilt on me for choosing the worse part. I expect you are nodding in solidarity as you read this.

Perhaps you can recall the gentle scolding of well-meaning youth pastors who, in an effort to coax us into the

45

practice of regular "quiet times," used this passage to illustrate the futility of busyness and the nobility of having a devotional time with God. Point taken.

Upon further examination, however, there is more going on here with the sisters from Bethany, and Jesus wants us to understand. Martha was not missing out on the best because of her busyness. She missed it because of her *fretfulness*.

In *lectio divina*, we begin with *lectio*, the first stage of the process: *we read the text with the goal of simply listening to it rather than analyzing it.* The Word speaks, we listen and receive, taking special care to ignore all of our presuppositions about what God might want to say to us, and letting the living Word speak afresh to us.

Mary and *Lectio*

Mary of Bethany shows us that this attentive, listening posture can be assumed in the midst of life. Granted, she has the advantage of receiving the words of Jesus as he speaks to her in person, right there in her home. Let's not let our envy of her keep us from seeing what's really going on. She is listening to the Word in the midst of her ordinary life, and in doing so is affirmed for what she doesn't do (worry) as well as what she does do (listen to Jesus).

If we want to be better equipped to defeat distraction and avoid surface spirituality, Mary demonstrates a very helpful principle: say yes to listening, say no to worrying. We know that worry bogs our souls down, along with its next of kin, *fear*. When worry takes over, faith and hope are squelched. Our bodies are affected as well—stomach pain, headache, cold sweat, trembling, to name a few of its symptoms. Worry and fear are to life as pitch darkness is to a child stumbling for the light switch—it paralyzes, confuses, and leaves us feeling utterly lonely.

Jesus' correction to Martha wasn't that she should stop taking care of people, or stop serving others, or stop making her home a welcoming place. His correction was to a woman who was being driven by her worries. Her worries were keeping her from what was best—the presence of Jesus.

Mary's Choice

It's easy for us to elevate Mary of Bethany to the level of sainthood, sitting there, as she is, calmly soaking up Jesus' words. But she surely has her own set of worries. We know she has a brother, Lazarus, who was there at dinner with Jesus, the same Lazarus who died not long after and was raised back to life by Jesus. There's at least an even chance that Mary was already aware that Lazarus was ill. That possibility would certainly be worrisome. Maybe Mary has her own little family, a husband, a child, giving her all kinds of natural and imagined reasons to worry. Life couldn't have been easy for women in that day; worry would have been an understandable option for Mary.

She simply chooses a better way to deal with it. Mary recognizes that Jesus' words are not only Truth, they are Life. Whatever Jesus said to her, I'm confident his words assured her and calmed her. Mary listens rather than frets.

And Jesus makes an example of her, declaring that this is the best choice.

Mary of Bethany embodies the first stage of *lectio divina*, which is *lectio*, meaning simply "to read." Jesus speaks, and Mary takes it all in, letting his words wash over her without analysis or critique. When we are beset by worry about many things, we can make a choice that turns us away from anxiety's control and toward the life-giving words of Christ.

By contrast, her sister Martha, also a friend of Jesus, seems unable to break away from the concerns that plague her. When faced with a worrisome challenge, we often mentally chew things over and over, feeling we are *doing* something about the issue at hand; if we don't ruminate on the problem, how will it ever get solved? Ours is a culture of doing, and we still resist any suggestion toward not-doing. It goes against our nature (our *fallen* nature, I would add) to stop doing and listen.

Listening to Jesus is a safeguard against paralyzing worry, resulting in the kind of peace we all long for and believe is possible. Stillness characterized Mary, even as agitation did Martha.

> Be still before the LORD
>> and wait patiently for him;
> do not fret when people succeed in their ways,
>> when they carry out their wicked schemes.
> Refrain from anger and turn from wrath;
>> do not fret—it leads only to evil.

For those who are evil will be destroyed,
>   but those who hope in the LORD will inherit
>   the land.
(Ps. 37:7–9)

Be still . . . wait patiently . . . do not fret. According to this psalm, contemplation—loving attention on God—can guide us back to hope in the Lord. It helps move my identification from Martha over to Mary, who chose the better part of listening to Jesus versus worry and anxiety. Replacing our frantic fretting with an intentional stillness and attentiveness to God is a skill, a practice that must be learned and repeated over time if we are to eventually become people who naturally choose what is best.

Our Choice

The lesson we learn here from the first of our Marys is very simply that we have the power to choose. At each moment throughout the chaos of our days, we are, whether we are cognizant of it or not, making choices about who or what is worthy of our attention. Even as I write this, my phone is vibrating, notifying me of some incoming message. It is shocking how quickly I will change my attention from the task at hand to that other message, even though my experience tells me the chance of it being critical at this moment is minimal.

As humans, we pride ourselves on our uniqueness among all of God's creatures; we have been given a will that is free. We can choose. And yet we easily give in to other forces that command our attention. The truth is, of course, that just because my phone buzzes, I do not have to respond to it.

And just because there is sorrow and suffering in the world, I do not have to let it dictate my thoughts and emotions about life in general. I do not have to give in to worry or anxiety; I can choose what is better. I can be aware of the reality of a broken world, but my attention is firmly on the One who speaks words of hope and healing. This is not mere positive thinking. This is choosing to believe what is true: "In this world you will have trouble," said our Lord. "But take heart! I have overcome the world" (John 16:33). When faced with the pain of the world, whether in my own home, in Baltimore, or around the world in Nepal, I can choose to listen to the life-giving words of Jesus, who assures me of his presence in the midst of it.

"I have set the Lord always before me," the psalmist says (Ps. 16:8 ESV). This is what Mary shows us. So we are not settling for pious platitudes in an effort to help ourselves feel better. We are walking behind Jesus, we are sitting at his feet, we are watching for his shepherd's staff ahead of us as we walk through the valley of the shadow of death. This is a mindful choosing of not only what is best but, for the follower of Jesus, what is essential.

We see Mary choosing Jesus … which means she rejects other things. She refuses to let everyday tasks distract her, and she refuses to let worry and trouble distract her. As Jesus said, there are "so many things" that we, like Martha, can choose to worry about, not recognizing that, in doing so, we are essentially admitting that the worries and anxieties have more power over us than Jesus does. If that is true, it is because we have given them that power.

Choosing a *lectio* posture is to listen at the feet of Jesus and refuse to give our minds and hearts over to worry and anxiety. The writer of Hebrews describes this as "fixing our eyes on Jesus" (12:2), giving an even stronger image of one who is determined to let nothing else command attention. Regular episodes of silent listening to God result in a profound stillness in the midst of life. It is a life that does not panic nor is it easily sent into frenetic agitation.

When we determinedly choose, like Mary of Bethany, to be satisfied with nothing less than the words and presence of Jesus—even when the worries of life buzz around our heads like summer mosquitoes—we make the best choice of all.

lectio for life

As a little child, I was a wad of anxiety. My worrying tended to hover around my parents' certain doom, that they would die and leave me alone. For example, if my parents ever went out on a date, the worrying would commence that morning. My tummy ached intensely, so fearful was I that they would have dinner, watch a movie, and die in a fatal car accident on their way home. My poor, long-suffering babysitter had to endure hours of my pitiful crying as I imagined myself growing up an orphan. Her response was always to gently coax me out of my bedroom and into the living room where she would read the New Testament to me (genealogies included). I hope my parents paid her well.

I grew to be a young mother with children of my own, and I proceeded to reverse the worry, fretting endlessly about the possibility of my own premature death. The fear I had as a child I now projected onto my children, and I constantly worried they would grow up motherless. Every odd spot on my skin convinced me I had melanoma; every migraine headache told me I had a brain tumor. Prayer and antianxiety medication have helped since, and I'm happy to say anxiety and fear no longer rule me.

But like everyone, I worry about finances. I can obsess over my college-aged daughter's future. I fret over my thoughtlessness and inability to keep in contact with distant relatives and the many other ways I fall short of the expectations I have of myself. And I do still get in a worry-snit now and then about the possibility of my husband, Cary, and me perishing while traveling—not so much because we would leave our children orphans (they are grown now), but because it necessarily means that someone will have to root through our "affairs" and discover what a rotten record keeper I am, and that our walk-in closet is a disaster, and . . . It's ludicrous, I admit, but I can put that fretter hat back on at a moment's notice.

Trivialities aside, there are the truly disturbing concerns that daily emerge as our world seems hell-bent on self-destruction. The word "terrorism" didn't enter my vocabulary until my early forties, when the 9/11 attacks changed the American mindset forever; now it is part of our daily lexicon. For the first time in at least two decades, we are hearing the phrase Cold War again on the nightly news. And the daily reporting of numbers related to the stock exchange has the power to send us into a gloomy funk. Our easy access to information is a blessing and a curse, and we have somehow granted our news media the power to construct our worldview.

Martha and I need to give more attention to Jesus' great sermon:

> Therefore I tell you, do not worry about your life,
> what you will eat or drink; or about your body, what
> you will wear. Is not life more than food, and the
> body more than clothes? Look at the birds of the
> air; they do not sow or reap or store away in barns,
> and yet your heavenly Father feeds them. Are you
> not much more valuable than they? Can any one of
> you by worrying add a single hour to your life? . . . So
> do not worry, saying, "What shall we eat?" or "What
> shall we drink?" or "What shall we wear?" For the
> pagans run after all these things, and your heavenly
> Father knows that you need them. But seek first his
> kingdom and his righteousness, and all these things
> will be given to you as well. Therefore do not worry
> about tomorrow, for tomorrow will worry about
> itself. Each day has enough trouble of its own. (Matt.
> 6:25–27, 31–34)

Sharing Our Anxiety

When we fret and spread the fear and anxiety to others, our ability to care for others is hampered. Researchers have discovered that it takes time, reflective time, for our brains to fully grasp the moral and psychological implications of any given situation. They have learned that the greater the distraction, "the less able we are to experience the subtlest, most distinctively human forms of empathy, compassion, and other emotions."[1] We see that this is true for Martha, because worry has led her to fear and selfish preoccupation. Anxiety has the power to take us into a downward spiral, away from the truth that we know, that God is good and all his ways are good. Worry grabs hold of our minds and hearts and drags us into territories that are alien, parched, and desolate. There is no life in the land of worry and fear, only a slow, insistent decay.

This is why Jesus hailed Mary for choosing something better. Quaker author Brent Bill notes that "Silence leads us to wait. Waiting leads us to the real presence of Jesus. The real presence leads us to holy awe. Holy awe leads us to a life lived out of spiritual silence. That life leads us to 'unhurried peace and power. . . . It is simple. It is serene. It is triumphant. It is radiant. It takes no time but it occupies all our time. . . . And when our little day is done we lie down quietly in peace, for all is well.'"[2]

Who Is God?

"Do not fret," the psalmist says, for "it leads only to evil" (Ps. 37:8). The opposite of fretting must logically lead to something good. I personally think Mary was not quietly listening to Jesus because she already knew stillness of soul—I think she listened because she knew it was the only way to attain stillness in the first place. When we listen to the words of Jesus with a heart that is open, fear is dissipated. Worry has no place. We are reminded that God is out to do us good.

> But now, this is what the LORD says—
>> he who created you, Jacob,
>> he who formed you, Israel:
> "Do not fear, for I have redeemed you;
>> I have summoned you by name; you are mine.
> When you pass through the waters,
>> I will be with you;
> and when you pass through the rivers,
>> they will not sweep over you.
> When you walk through the fire,
>> you will not be burned;
>> the flames will not set you ablaze.
> For I am the LORD your God,
>> the Holy One of Israel, your Savior.
>> (Isa. 43:1–3a)

We've been here at the family lake house for several days, enjoying holiday time together. As wonderful as that is, I had been looking forward to having some time for silent attention to God. This morning, I had an hour of peace to myself before the rest of the family awakened. With coffee in hand and a seat near the window looking out over the lake, the setting was ideal. The promise of stillness hung in the air, waiting on me.

Yet my mind instantly went into overdrive, chewing on all of the concerns I have for my children: the jobs they need, the changes in our jobs, my in-laws' health, and on and on. In that moment, a huge gust of wind came from the south, rattling the windows of our enclosed porch, and I watched as hundreds of the last of the fall leaves were blown, horizontally, from my left to my right, relocating from our yard into the lot next door. I remember a dear friend from Ireland once said to me, "There's nothing like a day at the sea to blow the cobwebs out." As I sat on the porch today, I received a vivid illustration of what has to happen in me before I can pay attention to what God has to say.

Lectio for Life

This is the role that *lectio* plays for us in the practice of sacred reading, *lectio divina*. We read the Word of God and listen to its teaching. The goal of *lectio* is to take us to God, to listen and not to analyze. It brings us to a place of stillness, away from agitation and distraction, so we can simply pay attention. We ingest the Word, taking it into ourselves as nourishment. How might we apply the same principle to life in general? How can we read life in search of God's instruction and presence? If worry is a major distraction, how can we combat it and be better attuned to the presence of Jesus in all things?

Our worries must be blown out and replaced by something better. There are a number of simple things I can do to get the process going. If the nightly news is shaping my perception of the world in a way that creates worry, I can take a break from it. If social media is taking command of how I view myself or others, I can fast from it. If paying bills before going to bed at night makes rest impossible, I can reschedule that most unpleasant task. If our culture of rampant consumerism breeds discontent in me, I can choose to resist the allure of Pinterest-perfect households or fashion-forward magazines. I have to determine to clear out the self-absorbed fretting and let God speak.

I read recently that if going to sleep naturally is problematic, one should avoid reading from an electronic device right before bed. Apparently, the light actually stimulates brain activity in ways that keep us from lapsing into that essential REM cycle of sleep. Stimulants make it difficult for our bodies and minds to quiet down. Shouldn't we assume the same of our souls? That what and who we listen to, what we watch, what we read, and what we ingest is going to have a direct effect on our inward state, and consequently, what emerges outwardly. Ultimately, what we listen to is what we will become.

Mary of Bethany chose to listen to Jesus, and whether she realized it or not, she was surely becoming more like Jesus because of it. Jesus demonstrated a stillness of soul. In the midst of a very busy and demanding life, he knew that stillness before God was essential if his ministry was to continue. He made a point of retiring to the mountainside, alone, after a full day of ministry, so that he might be still and listen to God. "How can I lead people to the quiet place beside the still waters if I am in perpetual motion?"[3]

"Be still and know that I am God" (Ps. 46:10). This is not merely a call for quiet contemplation; it is a call to the recognition that God is God, and we are not:

> God is our refuge and strength,
>> an ever-present help in trouble.
> Therefore we will not fear, though the earth give way
>> and the mountains fall into the heart of the sea,
> though its waters roar and foam
>> and the mountains quake with their surging.
>
> (Ps. 46:1–3)

The God we are talking about has no reason in the world to be worried, and he assures us that he is present and aware and capable of managing all that overwhelms us in this world. Tuning into that truth, that reality, and not giving way to worry will result in a greater stillness in our souls, bringing peace and assurance to others.

The Baptized Imagination

I've written elsewhere about the sacred Isle of Iona[4] and the spiritual practices of the early Celtic Christians there that have informed my own hopes for life with God and others. Iona is a place rich in Christian history, worship, and mission, and it is still today a destination for those who are seeking a fresh encounter with the Holy Spirit of God. The spectacular natural beauty of Iona—aquamarine waters, walking trails that lead to white beaches, and green, boggy farmland dotted with sheep—conspires with a restored Benedictine abbey to draw visitors into a spirit of awe and worship. I have been to Iona many times, and it never fails to produce this result.

Sometimes, when I'm at my desk here in the States, it occurs to me that in the midst of active, gratifying ministry, I haven't actually checked in with God in any meaningful or purposeful way. This is a familiar irony recognized by all who are in full-time Christian service. Sometimes the multitude of thoughts and concerns coursing through my mind are like fences I have to break through in order to be at the feet of Jesus . . . the email I just received from a troubled student, the worship service that needs planning, the preparation for next week's workshop on mentoring, the bill that needs paying, the dry cleaning that I keep forgetting to pick up, the long-suffering plant on my office windowsill that needs a drink of water. The distractions pull me away, like the undertow that tugs the unsuspecting swimmer out into dangerous waters.

But other times, when I have the will to resist the undertow, I go to Iona. In the midst of my anxious jag, I stop, take a breath, close my eyes, and use what C. S. Lewis calls the "baptized imagination."[5] It's the same tool we use on Good Friday when we imagine ourselves at the foot of the crucified Christ, and on Easter when we enter the empty tomb with the disciples. But in this case, I think of the quiet shores of North Beach on Iona, which I have often had completely to myself. I imagine myself standing on the shore. I breathe in the salty air; I listen to the waves. I watch a wild goose fly overhead, which Celtic Christians in more recent times see as a symbol of the Holy Spirit. And in my head, I hear a song, a lilting prayer that steals me away from my distractions and brings me to a still place before God:

> Here I stand, looking out to sea
> Where a thousand souls have prayed
> And a thousand lives were laid on the sand
> Were laid on the sand
> Years have passed, since they have died
> And The Word shall last
> And the Wild Goose shall fly
> Shall fly
>
> Here I stand, looking out to sea
> And I say a prayer
> That the Wild Goose will come to me
> That the Wild Goose will come to me[6]

It's not a bad thing to have a "prescription" for distraction, or to use tools to help us release the grip of fear and worry. This one happens to be mine. Eastern practitioners might use a mantra; Christians call upon the Holy Spirit.

Psalms

We can't know precisely what Jesus said to Mary of Bethany that day in her home. But we can be sure that whatever he had to say was in cooperation with the Word of God as he knew it, memorized it, and taught it. As we do battle with a fragmented, distracting world that seems to care little about the things of the spirit, an absolutely sure and reliable source of help is found in Psalms. These were the prayers of Jesus, as well as many Hebrew generations before him. And the exhortation to turn to Psalms regularly is perhaps one of the most helpful that can be given.

The Psalms provide a solid place to stand when our worries call us away from the truth. They convince us our worries can be replaced with something better. Kathleen Norris spent nine months living among and praying with the monks of St. John's Abbey in Minnesota. Her eloquent reflections on praying through the Psalms betray their earthy humanity while maintaining their sacred purpose. "To your surprise," she says, "you find that the psalms do not deny your true feelings but allow you to reflect on them, right in front of God and everyone."[7] The Psalms speak to us in the midst of our worries, giving them voice so that we can move on and be with God.

"One sister told me that as she prayed the psalms aloud at the bedside of her dying mother, who was in a coma, she discovered 'how perfectly the psalms reflected my own inner chaos: my fear of losing her, or of not losing her and seeing her suffer more, of saying goodbye, of being motherless.' She found that the closing lines of Psalm 16—'You will show me the path of life, / the fullness of joy in your presence'— consoled her 'as I saw my mother slipping away. I was able to turn her life over to God.'"[8]

Sabbath

A final thought for our purposes here is that we have to let go of the notion that we are victims of a busy, distracted life and determine to honor the biblical posture of stillness and silence before God. "You are a free person," Christopher Jamison reminds us, "and you can choose how busy you want to be."[9] As we explore ways to pursue an attentive, focused life, we must begin the way Mary of Bethany began: choosing. We can choose what is better; we do not have to be victims of the expectations or pace of the world around us.

Jesus knew this was the better way, because he had learned it from the time he was a child. In his Jewish family, the principle of keeping the Sabbath would have been foundational in his life. "Remember the Sabbath day by keeping it holy. Six days you shall labor and do all your work, but the seventh day is a sabbath to the LORD your God" (Exod. 20:8–10).

The practice of stillness before God is not only something God commands, but it is also a gift he gives. He has given us the freedom to stop, to listen, to relinquish control and the anxiety that accompanies it, and to take in his life-giving self. "Don't just do something, stand there!" The reversal of that common phrase is a bit unimaginative, yet it is true. We have been given permission to ponder, permission from the Lord himself to enjoy the "better part."

 *Prayer*

Almighty God, who after the creation of the world rested from all your works and sanctified a day of rest for all your creatures: Grant that we, putting away all earthly anxieties, may be duly prepared for the service of your sanctuary, and that our rest here upon earth may be a preparation for the eternal rest promised to your people in heaven; through Jesus Christ our Lord.[10]

Amen.

Notes

[1] Nicholas Carr, *The Shallows: What the Internet Is Doing to Our Brains* (New York: W. W. Norton, 2010), 221.

[2] J. Brent Bill, *Holy Silence: The Gift of Quaker Spirituality* (Brewster, MA: Paraclete, 2005), 33–34.

[3] Eugene Peterson, *The Contemplative Pastor* (Grand Rapids: Wm. B. Eerdmans, 1989), 28.

[4] Tracy Balzer, *Thin Places: An Evangelical Journey into Celtic Christianity* (Abilene, TX: Leafwood, 2006).

[5] C. S. Lewis, preface to *George MacDonald: An Anthology* by George MacDonald, ed. C. S. Lewis (New York: HarperCollins, 2015), xxxvii–xxxviii.

[6] Iona, "Here I Stand," recorded 1990, on *Iona,* Open Sky Records, compact disc.

[7] Kathleen Norris, *The Cloister Walk* (New York: Riverhead Books, 1996), 92.

[8] Ibid., 100.

[9] Christopher Jamison, *Finding Sanctuary: Monastic Steps for Everyday Life* (Collegeville, MN: Liturgical Press, 2006), 17.

[10] *The Book of Common Prayer* (New York: Oxford University Press, 1990), 99.

chapter 4

resolution

The Abbey Message arrived in my mailbox at home earlier this week, a few days before my visit to the monastery this weekend. I am oblate of Subiaco Abbey, which means I have a sort of familial connection to the monks. Clearly, I'm not one of them, as I am a married, non-Catholic female. But my designation as oblate helps me identify with them in spirit by praying for them, praying with them as I can, taking heed of Benedict's Rule as another bit of wise input into my life, and reading their newsletter, *The Abbey Message*, to try to keep up with news at the monastery. I may not be a monastic brother, but I can play the role of distant cousin.

This issue of *The Abbey Message* includes the usual features: updates about the monks and their various projects, how the grape crop did this year, obituaries, the latest round of novices, a change in appointments. I'm glad to know these things. I tuck them somewhere in the back of my brain, trusting I'll have some time for small talk with the monks. I continue perusing the newsletter and notice an item that requires further examination. Buried in the text about how many young monks are off pursuing graduate degrees, there is a brief sentence saying that Father Hugh has a new assignment. I can't quite get my head around this—Father Hugh is apparently no longer at the monastery.

This is not good news, not from my selfish perspective, anyway. Father Hugh is the resident historian and organist at the Abbey and has had this role for decades. I always look forward to introducing him to students when I take them for a weekend at the monastery, as he is such a fine example of how service and intellectual pursuit can continue well into senior years. My students usually witness him playing the great pipe organ for Vespers, which delights them. And then they are treated to his guided tour of the monastery museum, about which he knows everything; his vast knowledge of the monastery has been published in a hefty volume that is sold in the guest house bookstore.

The thought of Subiaco without Father Hugh is a bit jarring . . . sort of like Star Wars without the Force.

So after arriving at Subiaco today, one of the first things I did was ask one of the brothers about Father Hugh. Brother Francis is a gracious soul, always available to help protestants like me navigate the Benedictine world. He explained that that the reason Father Hugh's not at the monastery is that Abbott Jerome has given him the assignment of priest to a small church in Altus, Arkansas. Father Hugh is well into his eighties and, incredibly, has never in his entire life as a monk and priest served in a pastoral role at a church. He has spent all of his life as a priest in the Abbey, and in nearly sixty years of religious life, he has never been a priest to a congregation of laypeople.

"So . . . how is it going for him?" I tentatively asked Brother Francis. With a grin, he said, "Oh, he says he's bored. Such a small congregation. Saying the mass, visiting folks . . . it's all good, but what he really wants to do is get out and do something, like mow the lawn." I can just hear Father Hugh saying this, the voice of a twenty-year-old in an eighty-year-old body.

I don't know Father Hugh well, but he's enough of a fixture here at the monastery that I find myself pondering this comment with great curiosity. Here is a monk, a priest even, who is given a very religious task to do, to be a priest for a small congregation. It makes sense for him to take this post, and he obeys, because that's what monks do. Part of their commitment to monastic life is that they will submit themselves to the wisdom and leadership of the Abbott, so they go where the Abbott tells them to go. And so he goes and does what he is trained to do and has done every day of his life (but in the setting of the monastery): he celebrates the Mass, sharing the consecrated body and blood of Jesus with the folk in Altus, he baptizes, he prays with people, he gives counsel. This is what priests do. But in his life as a monk, he does not only pray and study Scripture and spiritual writing. Monks do something else that he is not able to do in his new post. Apparently, there's nothing in his new job description that calls for manual labor.

I'm sure he's doing more office-y things, which is very different from his work at the monastery. He surely has church members who pepper him with expectations. All that "church work" can wear on a monk's soul.

At the monastery, manual labor is a big part of life. Whether it be teaching at the boys' school, or caring for the herd of Angus cattle the monastery owns, or tending to the landscaping on the grounds, or crafting pine caskets that will eventually hold each one of them, the monks each have a task, and those tasks are shaped by the value of *ora et labora*—prayer and work. Their work is their prayer, and their prayer is their work.

I wonder if Father Hugh longs to mow the lawn because that's really where his prayer happens. At the age of eighty-something, he is having to learn a whole new application of *ora et labora*. It is ironic that those of us in professional ministry—pastors, missionaries, chaplains, youth ministers—can find it hard to do the very thing we are teaching others to do: pray. The expectations others place on us and our own impossible expectations of ourselves make it a real challenge to feel okay about being still before God for any amount of time. Father Hugh may be letting us in on a secret: when "quiet time" eludes us, walking behind a mower, moving it in even stripes back and forth, works as well as any candlelit chapel.

Last night, during Vespers, the psalm of the day made me think about Father Hugh:

> Planted in the house of the LORD,
> they will flourish in the courts of our God.
> They will still bear fruit in old age,
> they will stay fresh and green,
> proclaiming, "The LORD is upright;
> he is my Rock, and there is no wickedness
> in him."
>
> (Ps. 92:13-15)

After sixty years of monastic life, Father Hugh is very "planted" in the house of the Lord, still bearing fruit, still green. I have no doubt that he will find ways to do what Martha was challenged to do—refuse to get spiritually paralyzed by the worries and concerns of his new congregation and find new ways of giving attention to what is better. He will find stillness in the midst of duty that will allow the words of Jesus to permeate his work in such a way that flourishing results. I'm sure he will settle in just fine, praying and working as effectively in a small Arkansas church as he has done for so long at the monastery on the hill.

And hopefully, soon, he'll also get himself a mower.

chapter 5

the second mary:
meditatio

So they hurried off and found Mary and Joseph, and the
baby, who was lying in the manger. When they had seen
him, they spread the word concerning what had been told
them about this child, and all who heard it were amazed at
what the shepherds said to them. But Mary treasured up all
these things and pondered them in her heart. The shepherds
returned, glorifying and praising God for all the things they
had heard and seen, which were just as they had been told.
(Luke 2:16–20)

It is the season of Advent. Tomorrow is the third
Sunday, and church services around the world will share
a common observance, the lighting of the Advent wreath
candles. Our small Anglican church will join in as well, just
as we have the previous two Sundays since Advent began.
However, tomorrow we will enjoy an additional tradition
after the service—a visit from St. Nicholas. The feast day

of St. Nicholas was actually last weekend, but our church had to postpone a week; apparently our "St. Nicholas" was out of town. In a small congregation, everyone has to be willing to flex a bit.

Advent is about waiting, which is something we all know about, and most of us do not enjoy. Waiting pushes all of the buttons in us that are wired for efficiency in an era when no one seems to have enough time. It requires patience, which we are especially low on. In a season that is supposed to be characterized by "comfort and joy," we are more likely to experience agitation and frustration. We eagerly wait for loved ones to come home for the holidays. We count the days until school gets out and the holidays begin. We wait in lines, long lines, to pay for the gifts we are buying. One Christmas morning, over twenty years ago, I finally got what my husband Cary and I had been waiting several years for: a positive pregnancy test. In the best of times, waiting has its rewards.

But the Hebrews—waiting and longing for the promised Messiah to come, watching and praying through many generations. To wait a lifetime for something is beyond our modern comprehension. (I get twitchy if my online book order doesn't arrive within the promised two days.) The Jewish people may not always have waited well, but in the end they had no other option. God would bring his Man in his own good time, and there was no choice but to wait it out.

During Advent, we "wait" with God's people for the Messiah, and we celebrate when he arrives on Christmas

Day. Modern artistic depictions of the nativity most often display a scene where all is calm, and all is bright—but really, how could it have been? The worried husband, the pathetic conditions, the astonished shepherds, and, eventually, the arrival of wise men after a very long journey . . . calmness may have actually been at a premium for the new family and their guests.

My childhood Christmases were marked by my grand-father's annual telling of a not-so-calm Christmas pageant. Every year, with a glint of mischief in his aging eyes, he would tell of the time he, as a young boy, played the coveted role of Joseph . . . and how the audience audibly gasped when the manger suddenly collapsed and the Baby Jesus doll spilled out and rolled down the middle aisle. Not an accurate portrayal of actual events, thank goodness, but the stress level might be a direct match. There was probably a bit of chaos on that "silent night."

"But," Luke says, signaling a change in the story's direction, Mary's response was different. The mother of the Son of God treasured and pondered all that was happening. While the shepherds sprang into action, spreading Good News "over the hills and everywhere," and excitement and nervousness were invariably present, Mary found a way to reflect and carefully consider these important events in her life—in all of humanity's life. Jesus' mother Mary is an excellent teacher when it comes to pondering.

Mary and *Meditatio*

The second "stage" or movement in *lectio divina* is *meditatio*, or meditation, in which we begin to digest the sacred text. We take in a word or phrase that catches our attention and ruminate on it, chew it up, ponder it. Mary applied the posture of meditation to her *life* as she "treasured all these things, and pondered them in her heart."

Every year, I endeavor to teach my undergraduate students about biblical meditation. On the day I first introduce them to the idea, they are treated to hard butterscotch candy, which I pass around and ask them to please pop in their mouths while I begin the class. Now, unless one is impatient or simply has no regard for dental health, chewing these things is not a tempting option. What makes them satisfying is that if you take a butterscotch candy nice and slow, you will enjoy that delightful buttery sweet flavor for many minutes. It will last for a good long time, until it is finally gone. In addition, while you have it in your mouth, there's really no practical way of eating anything else simultaneously. The hard candy requires all the oral faculties, with none available for other flavors or textures. Butterscotch candies were meant to be savored and enjoyed, rather than rapidly chewed up and swallowed.

That's meditation—sitting with a short passage of Scripture, chewing on it, digesting it, and letting it begin its work in us before we declare to the world what we've discovered.

Likewise, when we apply *meditatio* to all of life, we discover that there is wisdom in treasuring what we are experiencing, holding it quietly and closely as something valuable and precious, and then mulling over it and reflecting on the meaning of it all before we share it and inadvertently dilute its significance. I think this is what Mary did, treasuring these holy events, not letting them escape her. She carefully pondered their meaning, and she stored it all up for future use when her baby would become a man and would upend the world.

At the root of Mary's meditative response is silent humility, humble restraint. She does not use her prestigious position as the one chosen by God to bring attention to herself. She resists any temptation to fill in unhelpful words, but responds in silent reflection. Mary shows us that the critical moments of our lives call for a silent waiting and ruminating that, when done with the guidance of the Holy Spirit, lead us to holy understanding of what is happening in the world. This is the effect of the kind of silent pondering that is "the particular equilibrium of sound and quiet that catalyzes our powers of perception."[1]

This fits what we already know about Mary. Earlier in her story, at what is historically known as the Annunciation, Mary's contemplative spirit is evident in her response to Gabriel's message. Though the news that she has been chosen to give birth to the Son of God is unsettling, to say the least, Mary's reaction is not one of panic. She does have a question or two for Gabriel, but even there she shows great restraint. "How can this be?" carries a much different tone than "No fair!" or "Not me!" which is surely how I would have responded. Mary is hailed as faithful and obedient because she quietly accepts what she is called to do. She relinquishes the rights to her life and body and does so without complaint: "Behold, I am the servant of the Lord; let it be to me according to your word" (Luke 1:38 ESV).

I am sometimes guilty of knee-jerk responses to the events of my life. When something amazing, or funny, or memorable happens, my phone is at the ready; I snap a photo and immediately post it to social media. I don't always take the time to consider if this is something I really need to share with the world.

More importantly, when a problem arises in my life, I am often too quick to rush to solutions. Ideas come tumbling out of my mouth, and a plan springs into motion before I take the slightest care in asking, "How is God leading here?" or "What role is my ego playing in this situation?" or "How urgent is it that I respond right now?" or any number of reflective, meditative types of questions that can lead me to a wiser response.

Treasuring and pondering before we react in a situation is just common sense, but it goes against our natural instinct to react. James, the brother of Jesus, agrees: "Know this, my beloved brothers: let every person be quick to hear, slow to speak, slow to anger; for the anger of man does not produce the righteousness of God" (James 1:19–20 ESV). Perhaps this is what Jesus was talking about when he suggested that we turn the other cheek when someone strikes us. Taking another hit ourselves is better than immediately retaliating, for Jesus knows that such a thoughtless reaction rarely turns out well; escalating anger tends to be the end result. When we are dealt a blow, it is tempting to react in kind, to defend ourselves and take things into our own hands. Like Peter, we can be too compulsive, and before we know it, someone's ear gets chopped off. It is risky to let enthusiasm run ahead of wisdom.

Mary's Treasure

Taking a meditative approach to life also helps us acknowledge the importance of that which is unseen. We live so much of our lives on a temporal plane, giving a tremendous amount of weight to tangible things that quickly pass away. Mary's son grew up to teach about this very thing, how to rightly balance the stewardship of earthly things with the greater, transcendent truths of God that must be our foundation:

> Do not store up for yourselves treasures on earth, where moths and vermin destroy, and where thieves break in and steal. But store up for yourselves treasures in heaven, where moths and vermin do not destroy, and where thieves do not break in and steal. For where your treasure is, there your heart will be also. (Matt. 6:19–21)

To treasure what is unseen and incorruptible over what is visible and temporal is a call to every Christian. When Jesus

79

preached this to the masses, I wonder if he thought of his mother, who may well have taught him this truth herself, having practiced it throughout the puzzling events of her own young life.

Some twelve years after Jesus' birth, we see Mary treasuring and pondering again. She is rightly disturbed—maybe even frantic—at the disappearance of her son after the family trip to Jerusalem. "'Why were you searching for me?' [Jesus] asked. 'Didn't you know I had to be in my Father's house?' But they did not understand what he was saying to them. Then he went down to Nazareth with them and was obedient to them. But his mother treasured all these things in her heart. And Jesus grew in wisdom and stature, and in favor with God and man" (Luke 2:49–52).

Luke tells us, his readers, that Mary and Joseph were confused by Jesus' response. There were surely many moments, as there are for all parents, when Mary's most unique son said or did things that were a mystery to her. But Luke chooses only to tell us that as his mother, in the midst of the confusion, Mary opted to treasure it, mystery and all. She knew she didn't understand and that treading wisely and prayerfully was the best course of action—as it should be for all of us who are given the humbling task of raising a child. This approach served her and her son well, for Luke confidently proclaims that Jesus grew in all of the ways we all want our children to grow: in wisdom (character, humility, obedience to God), stature (physical well-being), and favor with God and with others (healthy relationships).

Jesus grew in these ways because his mother showed him how. Could it be that Mary's meditative approach to life is one of the reasons God chose her over others to bear his son? Had he grown up learning to react impulsively to life, versus responding reflectively, his response to God on that grim night in the Garden of Gethsemane could, perhaps, have had a very different tone. If he had not learned to wait and reflect, would that intimate moment with God have happened at all?

Our speculation must be limited here. What we do know is that Jesus, in the face of certain death, did not lash out in self-defense. Rather, following the pattern of his mother before him, he relinquished the rights to his own life so that God's purposes would be fulfilled. "Not my will, but thine." The echo of Mary's words—*let it be to me according to your word*—can be heard in the words of Jesus.

Mary's decision to ponder and treasure all that was said to her and done through her resulted in a deep humility of spirit. Her example challenges me to do the same, to remember that there is always more going on than meets the eye. That to wait and ponder is a wise course of action in the midst of change and mystery, and that it will result in taking greater care before I thoughtlessly react to intense situations. If I would make the effort to truly treasure the events of my life, in the moment and no matter how confusing, I will be better prepared should I find my own soul being pierced one day.

Note

[1]George Prochnik, *In Pursuit of Silence: Listening for Meaning in a World of Noise* (New York: Doubleday, 2010), 293.

meditatio for life

Carry some quiet around inside thee. Be still and cool in thy
own mind and spirit, from thy own thoughts, and then thou
wilt feel the principle of God to turn thy mind to the Lord
from whence cometh life; whereby thou mayest receive the
strength and power to allay all storms and tempests.

—George Fox[1]

There is a scene in the film adaptation of *The Return of
the King* that makes me teary no matter how many times I
see it. Gandalf and his hobbit-charge Pippin have found a
brief moment of safety in the midst of the assault on Minas
Tirith. With great boulders being catapulted toward them,
arrows flying, and fellow soldiers falling all around, they
engage in this brief exchange:

> **Pippin:** I didn't think it would end this way.
> **Gandalf:** End? No, the journey doesn't end here.
> Death is just another path, one that we all must take.

The grey rain-curtain of this world rolls back, and all
turns to silver glass, and then you see it.
Pippin: What, Gandalf? See what?
Gandalf: White shores, and beyond, a far green
country under a swift sunrise.
Pippin: Well, that isn't so bad.
Gandalf: No. No, it isn't.[2]

While this particular conversation is not part of Tolkien's
original material,[3] it is an insightful addition by the screen-
play writers, for it gives us deeper insight into the humble
wisdom of Gandalf. It is a wisdom that we can only surmise has come from many a year of smoking his pipe and
pondering life in Middle Earth.

He has evidently pondered the reality of death and the
truth of an unseen glory that awaits ... and it has taken away
his fear. It has given him clarity and peace that transcends
the battle around him. His ability to think deeply about
the way things really are results in a view of death that has
changed from something to be intimidated by to something
that "isn't so bad." It's a fictional, yet profound example of the
fruit of *meditatio*, of pondering and treasuring. And while
there's no overt evidence that Gandalf is looking through
Christ-tinted lenses, we know that Tolkien indeed was.

Meditatio for Life

Of all of the stages of *lectio divina*, *meditatio* depends most
on the practice of silence. It is a necessary component of

all contemplative work, but here is where it is most prominently featured. Meditation can only do its best work in us when we are quiet enough to listen and carefully digest what is at hand. Whether it be in the pondering of holy Scripture or of the elements of our own lives, silence is essential. I, for one, can do without Gandalf's pipe, but his silent, pondering image resonates with meditation and provides a bit of a picture of what we're after.

"Silence is the door to the soul, and the soul is the door to God."⁴ Father Christopher Jamison, formerly of Worth Abbey, is a Benedictine monk and is well-versed in the practice of holy silence. In recent years, Father Jamison did an experiment with silence, filmed by the BBC. He invited five people to his monastery in England with the goal of teaching them the value of silent meditation and encouraging them to incorporate silence into their everyday lives. Watching the documentary, I was gripped by the difficulty these busy, contemporary adults had with settling down and not-doing, not to mention their resistance to the long periods of silence that were enforced by the monastic community.

As the participants wrestled with their own resistance, they gradually, over time, recognized the significance of that resistance: if silence is the door to the soul, then we had best be prepared for whatever we discover there. And that is a terrifying prospect. Most of us have an inkling of the darkness that can be found when we really take a look into our souls and, if honest, would prefer to just leave it be. Even those of us whose deepest intentions are to live as faithful Christ-followers know that our souls are in need of perpetual cleansing, and that takes courage.

Silence brings us face-to-face with who we really are. "Fear of disappearing, of the stillness of eternity lurking in the recesses of silence is . . . a reason that individuals like to hear themselves talk, and turn on a television the moment they walk into an empty room."[5] If we fill our lives with noise, it will be easier to ignore the darkness within.

Silence is intimidating because it threatens our self-importance. If I am silent, that means I am not talking, which means I am not voicing my opinions or getting my own way. In the United States, one of our most dearly held values is the right to speak freely, which is, in and of itself, a privilege that must be protected. It is possible, however, that the right to speak can, when taken to an extreme, hold more value than the people who are affected by what is said. Just because I *can* say something doesn't mean I *should*. Silence is threatening if we equate it with the neutralizing of our own voice or opinion.

If silence leads to the soul, and the soul leads us to God, then there may be even more reason to be concerned. Facing the depths of our soul is one thing; encountering the Almighty is altogether more daunting. When pressed, we might prefer a comfortable chat with God, the kind that comes in the midst of warm fellowship on a Sunday morning. But being still and silently attentive to God is to be open to the possibility of the violence of a burning bush or the chill of a still small voice—or, even more disturbing, no real "experience" at all. Our God is not one to be cornered, nor does he cater to our whims. To enter into silence is to enter into the kind of mystery that puts us in our proper place and allows God to be in his.

I see this kind of trepidation on the faces of my university students when they join me for a guided afternoon of silence twice a semester. The busy life of a college student (or a businessperson, or a pastor, or a parent) is excellent camouflage for creeping spiritual viruses. In silence, there's a very real possibility that the Holy Spirit will shed light on dark places. What if he tells me something I don't want to hear, or wants to discuss that thing I've been shoving to the back of the closet for years? Too often, we give the voice of denial more volume in our lives than the voice of the Holy Spirit.

Yet I also see the healing balm of silence when I take adults to the holy Isle of Iona in Scotland. On this tiny island, where there are very few automobiles and a blessed absence of shopping malls and movie theaters, our thirsty souls are able to drink in the silence in long, satisfying draughts. Likewise, when I take students through a weekend at Subiaco Abbey, they are surprised at how the silence and space there is like being enfolded in a downy comforter. The silence "isn't so bad at all." In fact, they usually leave the monastery wanting more, having had time to ponder God's Word and their lives without interruption.

Though I have led these kinds of experiences many, many times, I still have to fight my doubts before each one:

What if the group reacts negatively to silence? What if this time they rebel and resist, and the whole thing becomes a joke? Yet this never happens. *Never.* Because every time God meets us in his way and on his terms. With the help of the Spirit, fears are overcome, anxieties are calmed, and we all taste a bit of shalom in a new and life-giving way.

If we are to live in the depths of the abundant life with Jesus, we need to concede that he has actually given us permission to ponder, and that the world in its frenzy will go on without us—quite well, as a matter of fact. Mary's humility teaches us this. The humility that is forged in silence moves us from our compulsive possession of our lives and convinces us that we are not the managers of the universe. God is, and he does not slumber nor sleep.

Mary, the one chosen to be the mother of God, freely and humbly stepped out of the limelight, so to speak, to digest the events of her life—surely I can do the same. If Jesus, as busy and important as he was, found silence to be essential, it should probably be a clue for me to follow suit.

Making Sense of It All

I often wonder if God allowed the Israelites to wander for forty years for this exact reason. Their deliverance, their disobedience, and God's provision needed to be carved into their brains, not unlike the commandments that were carved into stone. Forty years would certainly create some space for pondering. We read God's exhortation to his people over and over—*remember.* They needed to constantly remember all the ways he helped them and delivered them. *Ponder, treasure, make this story part of who you are. Do not forget.*

All of us have had the experience of walking from one room to the next, only to be completely stymied as to why we made that move in the first place. Why am I here? What was I trying to do? I heard recently that there's a physiological reason this happens, that doorways serve as an "event boundary" that essentially files the episodes from the previous room away into a particular category. When we move into a different room, we've moved into another category, and it's hard to find the stuff from the previous category.

That's exactly how I feel about so much of my life that goes unprocessed. I go from one thing to the next, day after day after day, accumulating experiences but not amassing wisdom from those experiences. I have to take the time to ponder and make some sense of it all, to internally digest what has just come so that I can absorb some of the nutrition available to me. Anyone who has ever attended a conference knows what I'm talking about. Workshops, seminars, a packed schedule of speakers . . . it's overwhelming how much information comes our way. I sometimes feel that any helpful information I've gleaned at a conference must get absorbed by the airport scanners before I fly home, because I sure have trouble ever retrieving it. The reason? I've taken little or no time to ponder it all and find a permanent residence for it in the recesses of my mind and heart.

Write It Down

In the same way we make lists in order not to forget what we need to do, there is wisdom in putting pen to paper as a means of helping us process life in meaningful ways. The popular notion that "Jesus didn't journal" can take us off the hook if we're looking for a way to explain our aversion to writing. But what if Jesus did write in something like a journal? There are all kinds of things he did that Scripture doesn't record.

What matters is that if we are to figure out how to be attentive to God rather than distracted, and writing in a journal could be a helpful thing, then we should do it. If you haven't tried it, or your practice of journal writing has lapsed, I urge you to try again. I have no doubt that if Mary could have done, she would have been a journaler, because the point of pondering and treasuring is to get to the true meaning of things, to see the world as God sees. Putting words on paper makes them tangible and real, rather than shapeless ideas that float about in our minds. I have witnessed the value of this kind of reflection repeatedly, but never so profoundly as during a recent trip to Germany with ten university students. It is one thing to record the delightful discoveries of German culture; it is another to process the horrors of Dachau concentration camp after a visit. Writing gave the students a vehicle to sort out the conflagration of despair and hope that was Dachau.

Many, many times my journal-pondering has brought clarity to me when trying to understand the visible and invisible events of my life. My journal is an expression of prayer, not unlike the Psalms were to David and others.

This kind of meditation can take so many different forms. I know people who meditate and ponder by writing songs. I have other friends who find that a blank page and a box of crayons are wonderful tools for helping them treasure the events of their lives and the words God speaks to them. In addition to my journal, I've discovered that the other tool essential to my pondering is a camera.

On a recent trip to Ireland, I decided that I would forgo a camera and instead try to see my surroundings as they are, instead of through a lens. My logic was that I had taken plenty of pictures on previous trips to Ireland; I had no need to take the same pictures all over again. But my experience of Ireland that time somehow felt incomplete. Near the end of that trip, I realized that, for me, taking and preserving pictures is part of processing an important experience.

In addition, the subsequent viewing of those pictures over and over after the event made me continue the pondering process. My camera helps me see things differently, ponder them more fully through the pictures I take, and solidify those experiences in my memory. Rather than removing me from an experience, my camera actually helped me focus better. So now I know. No matter how many times I've been to a given place, I will always bring my camera.

Pondering with Others

Mary seemed to be an excellent internal processor, but for a lot of people, that is not what comes naturally. My husband and I are a study in opposites. Pondering comes a bit easier for me; I have many quiet conversations in my head. But Cary is one who does best when discussing ideas and addressing problems verbally. He is most definitely an external processor, explaining that "if it's in here (pointing to his head), it needs to come out here (pointing to his mouth)." We laugh about this, because it's always so obvious when he is entering into his processing mode. He talks and talks.... I listen and ask questions. It's all good, and it works for us.

External processing and verbal discussion are not contrary to pondering and treasuring. For some of us, *meditatio* is best done in the company of a trusted friend, a counselor, a spiritual director. Yes, silence is essential to pondering. But letting someone else give input can be just the thing to help us make sense of what God is saying to us afterward.

For a couple of years, I was part of a discernment group, a small group of colleagues that gathered weekly in my campus office for the purpose of helping each other listen to the voice of God in our lives. One of us would come prepared to present a situation in which God's direction was especially needed; a personal conflict of some kind, a seemingly unfulfilled request or pursuit, a place of spiritual confusion ... any kind of issue, big or small, was welcome.

The rest of us would silently and attentively listen to the other person talk for a few minutes, giving the group just what we needed to understand the question that was being tackled. We would then ask her some clarifying questions, giving her some time to further process. All of this was done with humble reliance on the Holy Spirit to guide and direct. And most every time, clarity and peace was the result.

> Quakers call the presence of the Holy Spirit working within us a 'sifting silence.' It separates the worthwhile from the worthless. Since we sometimes confuse those two—we may know what we value, but what we value may not be valuable. . . . Holy silence is a way of exploring the deep riches of the interior life, including the soul's discomfort with its failings, and asking God for help.[6]

It's Just Not That Easy . . .

Sometimes the circumstances in our lives make this ideal very, very hard to attain. When there are family members who depend on us, sometimes to an extreme but necessary degree, the suggestion to seek silence and space can be laughable, seemingly impossible. But pondering and treasuring need not require great spans of either silence or space. It might feel, at times, like we are trapped in a dark cave—a newborn requires every bit of our energy, our jobs become unreasonably demanding, an aging parent needs our extra care. In such times, the presence of an understanding friend can help us locate the small spaces where light creeps in.

My husband, Cary, has been my champion, urging me to seek silence and space when I need it. (Note: He has also learned that I'm a good deal easier to live with if I've got some space to ponder and be with God.) Whether this means my taking a Saturday afternoon to quietly read and write at a coffee shop, or going away to the monastery for a weekend of silence, or just hibernating in our study for thirty minutes here and there, he has fully supported me in this priority.

My friend Kim regularly asks me, "How are you and Jesus doing?" A pastor friend whom I see quite infrequently will nonetheless refuse the superficial pleasantries and ask me, "How is it with your soul?" Apparently, it takes a village to keep me on the path away from superficiality and toward the deeper things of God. And then there's Mary. We learn about meditation through her, but also through her son, whom she taught. Jesus is now our Master Teacher.

> Do not store up for yourselves treasures on earth, where moths and vermin destroy, and where thieves break in and steal. But store up for yourselves treasures in heaven, where moths and vermin do not destroy, and where thieves do not break in and steal.
> (Matt. 6:19–21)

Prayer

Almighty and everlasting God,

Who, of thy tender love towards mankind,

Has sent thy Son, our Saviour Jesus Christ,

To take upon him our flesh,

And to suffer death upon the cross,

That all mankind should follow the example of his

great humility;

Mercifully grant,

That we may both follow the example of his patience,

And also be made partakers of his resurrection;

Through the same Jesus Christ our Lord.[7]

Amen.

Notes

[1] George Fox, quoted in J. Brent Bill, *Holy Silence: The Gift of Quaker Spirituality* (Brewster, MA: Paraclete, 2005), 52.

[2] Chapter 38, *The Return of the King*, directed by Peter Jackson (2003; Los Angeles: New Line Home Video, 2004), DVD.

[3] It would appear that the screenwriters did use text from Tolkien's *Return of the King*, but adapted it for this particular scene in the movie. The original text is found in the chapter "The Gray Havens," and is as follows: "And the ship went out into the High Sea and passed on into the West, until at last on a night of rain Frodo smelled a sweet fragrance on the air and heard the sound of singing that came over the water. And then it seemed to him that as in his dream in the house of Bombadil, the grey rain-curtain turned all to silver glass and was rolled back, and he beheld white shores and beyond them a far green country under a swift-sunrise."

[4] BBC, "The Big Silence," documentary hosted by Christopher Jamison, aired December 15, 2010.

[5] George Prochnik, *In Pursuit of Silence: Listening for Meaning in a World of Noise* (New York: Doubleday, 2010), 290.

[6] Bill, *Holy Silence*, 46.

[7] Church of Ireland, *The Book of Common Prayer* (Dublin, Ireland: Columba, 2008), 268.

rumination

Tonight I attended Vespers, a service that happens every evening at the monastery. The great bells ring every night—"dong . . . dong . . . dong . . . dong"— repeatedly for the five minutes before the hour of seven, calling all to prayer.

It's a perfect first exposure for folks who've never visited a monastery before, because at Subiaco Abbey, it is a sung service. Music has a way of rounding off the edges of the cynical or suspicious constitution. And it is chock-full of Scripture, which puts us at ease. We sing the Psalms, back and forth, antiphonally, like two sets of opposing fans at a European football match, in a call-and-response pattern. It requires utmost attention so you don't stand at the wrong time or sing with the wrong group. But knowing these monks, they don't believe that's the worst that could happen. They are quick to smile, are eager to help us get back on the right page, and seem genuinely delighted that we're willing to give it a try. It is a lesson in humility, for sure.

My favorite part of the service is the repeated singing of the "Gloria" together: "Glory be to the Father, and to the Son, and to the Holy Spirit; as it was in the beginning, is now, and will be forever, Amen." This is sung several times in the service, in between each psalm. The monks always bow for the first phrase, adoring the Trinity. It's like we're all saying thank you to God for that wonderful bit of soul-nourishing Scripture. It's the bowing that speaks profoundly to me, because when we bow, we speak profoundly to God. It's body language in its holiest expression.

After the singing of the Psalms, one of the brothers comes forward for the appointed Scripture reading, followed by several minutes of silence for the purpose of reflection. This is helpful for me, not only because it's growing harder to retain information as the years go by, but because I really do want the Word to do its transforming work in me. I have been to very many worship services that give a polite nod to Scripture but too quickly move on to the next thing—and halfway through that next thing, I find I've already forgotten what the passage was, much less had it take root in my heart and mind.

Tonight's reading was from the Gospel of Matthew, the parable of the net, found in chapter eight. Jesus has been teaching his friends about the kingdom of God, using lots of colorful metaphors to help them understand: a sower, a mustard seed, a treasure hidden in a field, and such. The last metaphor, the one featured in tonight's reading, starts out in a generous tone: a net is let into a lake and brings in all kinds of fish. "All kinds!" my mind silently replies. "Yes, everyone is welcome!" I love the image. A gargantuan net filled with every kind of fish in the sea, one of which looks just like me. But then Jesus' tone takes a sharp turn, and there is a definite sorting of all those kinds. Jesus makes no apologies: some will be in, some will be out. And those who are out face a grim situation indeed.

Brother Matthias read this passage tonight and then calmly sat down. In fine Benedictine form, we sat as well, in order to ponder the Word. *Silence.* But internally, I was squirming. "These are hard sayings," my head said, struggling to receive them in peace. I've heard this Scripture many times before. But I have escaped the hard sayings easily, moving on to the next thing. If I want to avoid the many conundrums that are encountered in Scripture, I simply give myself permission not to ponder. I can turn my attention to a more pleasant distraction than dealing with the reality of Jesus' words.

Yet the Holy Spirit does not give up and will keep inviting us to engage. So instead of mentally moving on to something else, I responded to that invitation and dove right into it, discomfort and all. After just a few short minutes in silence, I discovered that instead of being perplexed (*where is grace in this scenario?*) or despairing (*will the end of the age really include a fiery furnace for some?*), I was given some very logical assurance: our righteous and just God will be exactly that. Righteous and just.

Recently, I had a fascinating discussion with my colleague Frank about capital punishment. Frank and I have known each other and worked together for years, so we can tell it like it is. I can share my views with him and know he won't think I'm a loon. So on this topic, I laid it out: I personally cannot support the death penalty because it is determined by fallen humans. It is too costly a decision to make when there's a fair chance the decision is actually wrong. By contrast, God is the perfect judge. If he is who Scripture tells us he is, then he will always choose right, always be fair, always be benevolent in his judgments. Our humanly-conditioned responses of "no fair!" will not be heard on Judgment Day.

I remember hearing Dallas Willard speak to our gathering of campus ministers from Christian universities around the country. Dallas was one of those people who, in the course of ordinary conversation, would humbly say or do things that were so profound I would feel the need to go take a nap afterward. On this particular day, Dallas was responding to that ever-popular question, "What will happen to those who never heard the gospel?" His answer not only helped me with that question, but it also brings me to my knees: "Whatever God does in the end, we will think it's a great idea."

Silent reflection will not guarantee all the answers. It will not turn us into brilliant biblical apologists. It is not intended to equip us better for theological debate. It will, however, bring us back to God, the God who is at all times and all places wise and just and good and fair.

Silence reminds me that I can only know so much. And that God knows it all.

chapter 8

the third mary: *oratio*

Six days before the Passover, Jesus arrived at Bethany, where
Lazarus lived, whom Jesus had raised from the dead. Here
a dinner was given in Jesus' honor. Martha served, while
Lazarus was among those reclining at the table with him.
Then Mary took about a pint of pure nard, an expensive
perfume; she poured it on Jesus' feet and wiped his feet with
her hair. And the house was filled with the fragrance of the
perfume.

But one of his disciples, Judas Iscariot, who was later
to betray him, objected, "Why wasn't this perfume sold and
the money given to the poor? It was worth a year's wages."
He did not say this because he cared about the poor but
because he was a thief; as keeper of the money bag, he used
to help himself to what was put into it.

"Leave her alone," Jesus replied. "It was intended that
she should save this perfume for the day of my burial. You
will always have the poor among you, but you will not always
have me." (John 12:1-8)

This passage takes us once again to Bethany, with
Jesus and his friends, Mary, Martha, and Lazarus. A dinner
is held in Jesus' honor, which seems appropriate, since Jesus

recently raised Lazarus from the dead. There was definitely something to celebrate.

At least four of them were friends, good friends, as the Gospel writer is careful to point out in John 11:3, 5, and 11. When I read these verses, I am once again envious of the sisters and their brother. What would it have been like to be friends with Jesus—to glean his wisdom, to talk about current events, to hang out with him? For now, I will have to be content with knowing only in part. One day, we will all know what it's like to see him face-to-face, to talk together as friends.

Martha is again serving, meeting the needs of the guests—but with no evidence of fretting this time. Lazarus is at the table with Jesus and presumably others, most likely the disciples. And our third Mary is again at the feet of Jesus. This is the familiar story of Mary of Bethany anointing Jesus' feet with expensive perfume, much to the chagrin of Judas, the thief.

When practicing *lectio divina* with Scripture, the next stage—*oratio*—brings us to the text a third time. This time, we ask God how we should respond to what we have heard thus far. Since *lectio divina* requires a slower pace of reading and a good bit of silence between each reading, by this time there is often a sense of the Holy Spirit's leading with regard to application of the text to real life. *Oratio* invites us to take the word or phrase that we've been meditating on in particular, and ask the Spirit to give us instructions in response.

We are, after all, instructed to "not merely listen to the word, and so deceive yourselves. Do what it says" (James 1:22).

If we apply the same principle as we ponder our lives, we should ask God the same thing: How am I to respond to this? What is it that God would have me do, now that I have seen what I have seen, now that I have heard what I have heard? It takes real internal strength to resist all other expectations, whether they come from well-meaning friends, popular culture, or our own quiet-but-critical voice. Everyone else will happily tell us what we should do. But it's God's voice we want to hear.

Mary and *Oratio*

Here Mary of Bethany shows us, by her actions, that she has done exactly that. To better grasp the importance of her example, let's review what we know about this Mary so far.

First, as we've already seen, Mary has had the opportunity to sit and listen to Jesus in a very intimate setting. She is not one of five thousand people on a hill—she is one of a limited number, limited by the size of her home, which we can safely assume is not especially large. Mary has a front-row seat, as it were, and is a member of a very exclusive audience, not only because it is her home, but because she is one of Jesus' special friends. This fact leads us to believe that Mary has likely had a number of opportunities to listen to Jesus in this way, perhaps many. I feel quite certain that Jesus was not only a friend to her; he was her spiritual director and teacher more than any other in her life.

Eugene Peterson believes there are two words that describe the Christ-follower: disciple and pilgrim. I suppose it was Mary's gender that kept her from officially being included in the biblical text as a disciple; the cultural norms of the day would have dictated that. But she behaves in ways that betray her true allegiance: she listened to Jesus, learned from Jesus, and pondered Jesus' words. She was likewise a pilgrim, for she has intentionally placed herself in Jesus' path.

For me, there is nothing more enriching to my soul than to listen to an expert speak about what he knows, and for him to speak in ways that challenge me, the nonexpert. This is especially true when the teacher's expertise is in spiritual matters, the things of God. But because I firmly believe that all truth is God's truth, I have often been moved to a greater love of God through the voices and talents of authors, musicians, and physicians whose faith (or lack of) is different than mine. A few years ago, Cary and I had the memorable opportunity of hearing Pulitzer Prize–winning poet Mary Oliver at a poetry reading. I don't know Mary's faith story. But her words brought us to the feet of God. Listening to an expert teach always leads to me to a sense of awe—amazement at the work of God, his presence in unexpected places, and his compassion for people, for me.

Even better is to learn from someone who not only knows a lot about God, but clearly knows him intimately. To be with such a person is like being with Jesus himself; and isn't that how Christians are to relate to each other and to the world?

Mary not only learned from Jesus and benefited from his teaching. She saw him perform a spectacular miracle. John 11 features the remarkable raising of her brother Lazarus from the grave. How does one process such a life-altering event? And it is not just a fantastic trick; it is a gift of life and love to her and to her sister and to all who were grieving Lazarus's loss.

Her life was forever changed after that unprecedented event. Every choice she would make from then on would be in response to the miraculous presence of Jesus in her life. The episode at hand—the dinner in honor of Jesus—provides evidence that Mary, in the spirit of *oratio*, recognizes that for all Jesus is and all he has done in her life, a response is required of her.

On the afternoon of their dinner party, was she consumed with her thoughts of how to truly honor Jesus? Was something to be done, in addition to the dinner, to express her gratitude and appreciation for him? (Some might surmise that Mary was merely trying, once again, to one-up Martha, who was, once again, faithfully at work, while Mary found a way to command Jesus' attention. I will leave that possibility for others to explore.)

Mary learns soon enough that her response to Jesus will not be popular. It's a lesson she learned earlier, when Martha criticized her for choosing to be with Jesus rather than helping her with the serving. And here, in the John passage, Judas complains that Mary is not using her possessions for the poor, but is choosing Jesus instead. I can identify with the pressure this brings to Mary. The expectations of others are formidable, especially when articulated by the lips of the faithful. When added to the expectations I have of myself, I can find myself in a real conundrum. What I "should" do and what I am "called" to do are not always the same thing.

Reverence

A university student I know was recently walking in downtown Tulsa on an especially cold night. As she and her boyfriend walked along, they passed a man, clearly homeless, on the side of the street. This student felt compelled to give a homeless man her coat (and it was a very nice coat). He hadn't asked for it. But there in the cold of the night, she knew she could not *not* give it to him; it would have pained her to keep it. She recognized humanity in him, maybe even the image of God. Her response was to honor him with her gift.

Judas believed Mary's extravagance to be completely out of order. It was, upon reflection, very much in order. Mary had carefully contemplated all that Jesus had said to her, and this was her response. Like my student friend, Mary could "not *not*" show her love to Jesus in this way. Her act of anointing Jesus' feet with expensive perfume betrayed the reverence and awe she had for him. Jesuit priest Karl Rahner said, "Ultimately the only adequate response to God is silent adoration."[1] With only six days to go before Passover, perhaps Mary somehow knew that Jesus' time with them was very, very short. The time to express her love and gratitude was now. "For in real charity one loves God for himself alone above every created thing and he loves his fellow man because it is God's law. In the contemplative work God is loved above every creature purely and simply for his sake. Indeed, the very heart of this work is nothing else but a naked intent toward God for his own sake."[2]

Mary, as much as anyone, recognized in Jesus the evidence of holy divinity. It's important to note that each time she is featured in Scripture, she is on her knees before Jesus: in Luke 10 she sits at his feet and listens; in John 11 she falls to her knees in desperate pleading on behalf of her brother; in John 12 she anoints his feet with perfume—a gesture of absolute worship and adoration.

The result of Mary's pondering was reverence. Reverence is an indicator of a deep respect for God, an awareness of his holiness, followed by a worshipful response. The anointing was for him alone, the only one in the room worthy of the honor. Mary chose to worship and adore Jesus in the most extravagant way she possessed. There was no expense too great, no gesture too grandiose for the amount of regard she had for him. She made this choice despite the disapproval of her peers. Mary shows us that when our attention is firmly fixed on Jesus and the ways he makes himself manifest in our lives, the first response is extravagant reverence.

The reverse, then, is true: when we are distracted and consumed by shallow living, our regard for Jesus will be the same—shallow.

Notes

[1] Karl Rahner, quoted in George Prochnik, *In Pursuit of Silence: Listening for Meaning in a World of Noise* (New York: Doubleday, 2010), 44.

[2] William Johnston, trans. and ed., *The Cloud of Unknowing* (New York: Image, 1973), 80.

oratio for life

As a self-identified Anglophile, I have a deep affection for all things British. I'm in love with the British countryside, British accents, British architecture, British history—put the descriptor "British" in front of a noun, and I'm in.

This includes the royals, of course. What is it about royalty that has us completely gobsmacked? That happens to be how I'm feeling at the moment. A gentleman we know in Killyleagh, Northern Ireland, has been given a special royal honor and will soon be visiting the Queen at Buckingham Palace to receive it. Our friend will need to prepare a bit for his meeting with the Queen—how to bow, how to address her ("Your Majesty" is the proper title)—all in an effort to properly communicate esteem and respect in a spirit of humility before the monarchy.

I'm more than a bit jealous. The closest I've ever been, maybe ever will be, to royalty was the day that the Prince of Wales's motorcade whizzed by us as we drove on the M2 in Northern Ireland. It happened before any of us in the car realized it; nary a wave was exchanged.

I think the longing we experience—temporally fed by fairy tales and stories of real-life dukes and duchesses—is for a kingdom that actually exists, that is at once now and not yet, and that we are being fitted for even as we speak. If we would pause to reflect on the reality of the kingdom of which we are citizens, and even more so, the king who has always ruled and will one day rule with every knee bowed before him, perhaps we'd be less satisfied with the charm of an earthly monarchy. Perhaps we would be more inclined to bow our knee to our Eternal and Only Wise King with an ever-increasing sense of loyalty and adoration.

This is what Mary of Bethany does in John 12. Without doubt, Mary knew Jesus as her beloved friend, and Scripture tells us he considered her the same way. But Mary's attentiveness and expression of sacrificial love tells us that she knew him to be so much more. Where we tend to sidle up to Jesus as our "Friend of Friends," Mary's gift of anointing perfume hearkens back to the Magi bringing extravagant gifts to the baby King of Kings.

Learning from Monks

Every fall, I take a small class of honors students to nearby Subiaco Abbey. As I mentioned earlier, I have a relationship with the monastery—I am an oblate[1]—so the Benedictine abbey has become another spiritual home for me. For my students, however, going to the monastery is like a cross-cultural experience; I might as well have put them on a plane and plopped them down in France. From the moment we arrive and they catch sight of the imposing Abbey church, their adventure of monastic discovery throws them a lot of curve balls. They soon learn that a real monk at a real monastery is quite different from whatever they had previously imagined him to be.

Our weekend retreat at Subiaco revolves around the monks' daily rhythm of prayer, to which the brothers warmly welcome us. I typically designate the earliest prayers, beginning at 6:30 A.M. on weekends, as optional. I know that college students are perpetually fatigued, so I want to be realistic about their ability to participate at that early hour. But, to my surprise, the majority of the group does indeed get up and attend that first service of prayer. They then stick around for the morning Mass that follows soon after. Noon prayers happen at 11:45, followed by a service of readings at 5:30 and Vespers at 7:00 P.M. The students attend them all, their level of engagement growing with each service. By the time we leave for home forty-eight hours later, they've gotten into the rhythm and feel as much at home in the once-strange setting as I do.

A few days later, we gather for one last class session together. I ask them to talk about what struck them most about their visit to the monastery. In every group I've taken, the response is the same: *reverence*. This seems to be the best word to describe their experience. After a weekend of joining the monks in prayer five times a day, experiencing the contemplative silence that is available at a monastery in the middle of the Ozark mountains, and observing a colony of men who have dedicated their lives to prayer and service, they are blanketed in reverence for God in a way that is radically different than anything they've previously experienced—even at a Christian university, where we worship together regularly and take the study of Scripture seriously.

And they welcome this reverence with open arms. They become sharply aware that reverence is something they need to have if they are to be fully open to God—to his mystery and grandeur, as well as to his friendship. They begin to consider the breadth and depth of their own personal engagement with a holy God. They are forced to consider the degree to which they are placing limits on their understanding of God and his character. And they become energized by the reminders they can know God as a friend, but a friend who is also a king.

Oratio for Life

Of course, it is easier to encounter holiness, to come to God in reverence, when there is a towering Abbey church in which to worship. Stained glass, a great gold crucifix, silence—it all points us to the holiness of God. And my students begin to consider how little there is in their daily world that visibly and intentionally points them to the holiness and majesty of God. They recognize that their own Protestant tradition has been relatively (and intentionally) low on symbol and fantastic architecture, and they find that there may be some space in their lives for such things . . . that artistic design and the use of color and material can play a legitimate role in pointing us to God.

Even so, a grand cathedral isn't a requirement for encountering God's holiness. For some, an ornate structure is too reflective of human effort, and it can even be a distraction. In that case, the cathedral of God's natural world is the obvious alternative and can be a place of worship for all who believe God to be the most skilled architect of all. Beauty leads us to the reverence of God, the author of beauty. So whether it is found in a silent sanctuary or at the foot of a spectacular mountain range, beauty is a channel of grace to us.

"Worship the LORD in the splendor of his holiness; tremble before him, all the earth" (Ps. 96:9). When did you last witness the kind of beauty that led you to wonder at the indescribable reality of God? Has there been anything in your life of late that made you step back and gasp, convinced that God was there?

Life demands much of us, to the degree that to talk of beauty and its meaning can seem laughable. I sometimes feel that the myriad of concerns rattling around in my brain is like the stacks and stacks of books that can so easily accumulate on my desk at work. Each one needs to get put back on the shelf, each one has a place, and they are not going to get there by themselves. I have to give in and put each away, and that takes my time and attention. But as I do, I find that I make delightful discoveries along the way—if, that is, I take time to read the titles, perhaps page through a few of them and rediscover what it is that I appreciated about them. I may even discover some annotations that reignite my thinking. Often, I will discover some sort of memento tucked between the pages—a train ticket, a postcard, a pressed leaf. Even in the midst of a daunting task like reshelving my books, I can encounter bits of beauty that transport me from the mundane to something almost sublime. Life is indeed demanding, but there are so many bits of it that are *numinous*—charged with meaning beyond itself.

To pursue beauty is not to turn aside from the reality of the brokenness of the world. Mary was essentially accused of that by Judas when he criticized her for giving the perfume to Jesus, rather than using its value to help the poor. Jesus set him straight, of course, reminding him of Mary's first allegiance, which was to him. When our souls are shaped by a robust appreciation for the holiness of God, our view of the needs of the world changes. When I begin to grasp that holiness, I see a world that can be redeemed, that can be made holy. I see that I am to be a partner in the redemptive process, and my pondering can turn into Spirit-directed activity.

The Reverence of Work

Our visit to the monastery also exposes us to a way of life that treats all of work with reverence. Again, we see this in the Benedictine value of *ora et labora*, which translates "prayer and work." The brothers don't see their lives as bifurcated into two categories, "prayer" and "work," but rather that prayer and work are all of a piece. Their cultivation of the grapes in the vineyard is as holy as their prayers at Vespers. They consider their work, whether it's in the woodshop or out in ministry in the nearby community or hosting guests in the retreat house, to be their prayer. And they consider their prayer, at morning, noon, and night, to be their work.

The early Celtic Christians in Ireland and Britain saw all manual labor as holy and worthy of consecration. The prayers that have been passed down over generations reflect an openness to collaboration with God that is refreshing and a model for any of us who find modern life to be a distraction to truly spiritual living. What if we habitually consecrated the tools of our day for God's use? The car is started, the computer is turned on, a child is bathed in a posture of reverence for God.

This is encouraging to all of us, for we all find our daily work to be very ordinary at times, perhaps even monotonous. Each of us questions the value of what we do, wondering if we are making a difference in the world at all. What if we habitually joined forces with Mary of Bethany, taking our daily work and "anointing" Jesus with it, humbly and reverently at his feet?

Higher Thoughts

Long ago, I was introduced to a man who would be a spiritual mentor to me—though I never actually met him in person. Our interactions came by way of the books he wrote, and they came to me midway through my own college experience. A. W. Tozer was a pastor and writer who shared, almost to the year, the same era as C. S. Lewis, each of them born late in the nineteenth century and dying in 1963. With a prophetic voice, Tozer called his hearers to a deep experience of God that was fueled by a more profound realization of his character.

Dr. Tozer helped me understand that "what comes into our minds when we think about God is the most important thing about us."[2] His book *The Knowledge of the Holy* invites the reader to the kind of adoration and adulation of God that Mary of Bethany knew and that the angels in heaven know. He passionately urged Christians to think higher thoughts of God: "Without doubt, the mightiest thought the mind can entertain is the thought of God, and the weightiest word in any language is its word for God."[3]

In the agitation of our days, our thoughts of God are not terribly lofty (if they are present at all). But a sweep through Tozer's chapters is an exercise of the heart and mind as worthy as any for the body. Tozer discusses the eternity of God, the incomprehensibility of God, the self-sufficiency of God, the transcendence of God, the holiness of God, the immutability of God, and more.

I remember reading an anecdote, inaccessible to me now but memorable nonetheless, about a friend of Tozer's, a student perhaps, who set about looking to find his teacher one day, and came upon him in a quiet garden place, prostrate, facedown on the ground in reverent prayer. This story was told as a way of graphically portraying Tozer's own understanding of God. Clearly, he had not tucked God into a tiny, manageable box. Tozer's response to God indicated something quite the opposite.

> The low view of God entertained almost universally among Christians is the cause of a hundred lesser evils everywhere among us. A whole new philosophy of the Christian life has resulted from this one basic error in our religious thinking.
>
> With our loss of the sense of majesty has come the further loss of religious awe and consciousness of the divine Presence. We have lost our spirit of worship and our ability to withdraw inwardly to meet God in adoring silence. Modern Christianity is simply not producing the kind of Christian who can appreciate or experience the life in the Spirit. The words, "Be still, and know that I am God," mean next to nothing to the self-confident, bustling worshipper in this middle period of the twentieth century.[4]

Mary of Bethany and A. W. Tozer are two voices in unison, urging us toward a higher view of God, and a higher response to who he is.

Teresa of Avila, a contemplative writer of the sixteenth century, would agree as well, evidenced by her recurring reference to "His Majesty."

In deepest humility, she prays, "May it please His Majesty to give us understanding of how much we cost him, of how the servant is no greater than his master."[5]

If we determine to gain that higher view of God, our problem of distraction will diminish. For as we learn to let the beauty of natural creation, the image of God in all humanity, and the work we do direct our thoughts ever more toward God, we will have no choice but to stand in awe at what is before us. Which is the most appropriate response to a holy God.

 *Prayer*

Risen Christ,

By virtue of your passing over from death to life,

Pour your Holy Spirit into our hearts.

Fill us with awe and reverence for you

And love and compassion for our neighbor,

For yours is the power and the glory,

Now and forever.[6]

Amen

Notes

[1] "Oblates are women and men who through association with a specific monastic community place their lives at the service of God while remaining at home in the world, fulfilling their obligations to their families and in their working lives. At the same time they have a particular vocation to be in places where God is present in the world." Notker Wolf, forward to *The Oblate Life*, ed. Gervase Holdaway (Collegeville, MN: Liturgical Press, 2008), 1.

[2] A. W. Tozer, *The Knowledge of the Holy* (New York: HarperCollins, 1961), 1.

[3] Ibid., 2.

[4] Ibid., vii.

[5] Teresa of Avila, *Selections from the Interior Castle* (New York: HarperCollins, 2004), 22.

[6] William Storey, *An Everyday Book of Hours* (Chicago: Liturgy Training Publications, 2001), 6.

reverence

I am once again at the monastery, this time with my friends and colleagues—Rod, Frank, Lisa, and Jen—on a staff retreat. Every January, we make a point of getting off campus for a couple of days to regroup before students return and another busy semester catapults us all into motion. The monastery is just right for our purposes; we need space to reconnect after the Christmas holidays, and we need a rhythm of prayer to enter into. As always, the brothers here are at their Benedictine best, demonstrating their core value of hospitality with warmth and humor.

And it is Epiphany! Each time we've joined the brothers in the choir stalls for the liturgy of the hours today, the readings and prayers have been all about celebrating the arrival of the Magi. Last night, as our group talked about how to best use this retreat time, we agreed that this afternoon would be a silent one for each of us. So I've found myself a quiet loveseat at the end of the retreat house hall and have tried to listen to God. I'm contemplating the Magi passage, Matthew 2:1–12, with the help of *lectio divina*.

"We saw his star," the Magi tell Herod, "and have come to worship him." That star has become a fixture of Christmas celebrations, whether sacred or secular. As I ruminate on something so familiar, I recognize how much significance I have previously missed regarding the star. Christmas after Christmas it appears, and without thought, I dismiss it as an inanimate player in the nativity, a mere object among many. It's a piece of the Bethlehem puzzle, along with a manger, some straw, and a cow or two.

Star-Gazing

It occurs to me that the star was not only a signal, a signpost that led the Magi to Jesus. It did not merely function as a great arrow in the sky. It led them to adoration, to reverence. The Magi didn't just want to *find* Jesus, they wanted to *worship* him. And I find myself pondering this in a new way: What if the star was somehow, by God's design, only visible to the Magi? If it had been a spectacular astronomical event, wouldn't Herod have already known about it? But no, he "and all Jerusalem" were disturbed when the Magi told him about it. What if the star was only visible to those who truly wanted to worship the Messiah?

In the course of my meditation, I didn't allow my mind to go too far down that rabbit trail, and I returned to pondering the idea of a star leading people to worship Jesus.

The third reading, *oratio*, called for me to ask God what this might mean for me. Was there a response I should make to this small bit of the passage that had acquired my attention? Nothing particular, only more questions: Is there a "star" somewhere in my life that is urging me to bow in worship? If there is, why am I not paying attention to it?

It's easy for me to point to all of the things that distract me away from God. I can lay blame at the feet of the easy target of busyness. Or my own fatigue. Or the needs of my family and friends, church, work. . . . It's shocking how much I may actually have in common with Herod, who was somehow blind to the vision of something that fairly shouted for his attention. So instead of just whining about my distracted life, I sat there in the quiet and pondered where the stars were. Where are the Spirit-placed attention-getters that I am not noticing, or swiftly passing over, or ignoring altogether?

One of the first stars that came to mind—ironically, because there are literal stars involved—was a fabulous picture taken by the Hubble telescope. It showed up on my Instagram feed just yesterday, and it actually contained countless stars. It is called "The Pillars of Creation." As I saw it, for a flash of a second, I did have a small "God thought"; my soul did sense a bit of a lurch Godward. But, as usual, my thumb continued to briskly scroll through the many other pictures on Instagram. I could have stopped, even for just another minute or two, to take advantage of NASA's description of this amazing interstellar phenomenon. It would have,

I'm certain, given me pause for worship. Next time I will take more time. Even a small picture on my phone has the power to direct my attention to God.

With this intriguing idea of "stars" in my head, I left the retreat house and walked outdoors. I've been to this monastery many times, yet with each visit I discover new things. This time, I took an unfamiliar path around the east end of the Abbey church, where I spotted a stone grotto with a fountain. Curiously, a stone kneeling bench was placed in front of the grotto. We protestants don't tend to place kneeling benches here and there; I was intrigued.

I continued walking around the Abbey until I reached the front stairs, which I ascended, and opened the big door into the sanctuary. I love the Abbey church; it is a holy place to me and to many, and I always make a point of prayerfully sitting there, the only person in a massive sanctuary on a quiet afternoon.

But today, just as I moved to sit in my usual front pew, something in my peripheral vision caught my eye. To my extreme right, where a small alcove dedicated to St. Benedict usually stands, was an artfully arranged nativity scene. The characters were all there, much larger in size than the nativities we typically encounter. It was a bit like looking at an exhibit in a zoo, to be honest. But because it was so beautifully done, I wasn't allowed to just stand and observe, like I do in front of the orangutan cage. The scene drew me in, and as I looked at each member of the holy family, at each visitor, at the angel above, the reality of their presence on earth gave me a jolt of wonder.

And there, in front of the scene, was a kneeling bench.

There was no escaping the allure of the bench this time. I knelt there and entered into the scene, along with the Magi who were "overjoyed . . . and they bowed down and worshiped him."

The Bethlehem star and the Subiaco kneeling benches are showing me today that there are opportunities for deep and reverent worship all around me, and I had best start looking for the signs. They are somewhat easy to spot as one wanders around a holy place like a church or a monastery. But what about the rest of this ordinary yet extraordinary earth? Is there a kneeling bench on my Instagram feed, pointing me to a mind-boggling Creator and creation? Is there one in the grocery line behind the woman with three small children? How about in the dormitory, or the classrooms, or the cafeteria on the university campus where I work? Could there be a star telling me that Jesus is there, and I should adore him?

Or am I carelessly scrolling past them?

chapter 11

the fourth mary:
contemplatio

Now Mary stood outside the tomb crying. As she wept, she bent over to look into the tomb and saw two angels in white, seated where Jesus' body had been, one at the head and the other at the foot.

They asked her, "Woman, why are you crying?"

"They have taken my Lord away," she said, "and I don't know where they have put him." At this, she turned around and saw Jesus standing there, but she did not realize that it was Jesus.

He asked her, "Woman, why are you crying? Who is it you are looking for?"

Thinking he was the gardener, she said, "Sir, if you have carried him away, tell me where you have put him, and I will get him."

Jesus said to her, "Mary."

She turned toward him and cried out in Aramaic, "Rabboni!" (which means "Teacher").

Jesus said, "Do not hold on to me, for I have not yet ascended to the Father. Go instead to my brothers and tell them, 'I am ascending to my Father and your Father, to my God and your God.'"

Mary Magdalene went to the disciples with the news:

Of all the stories of Jesus, this one has always endeared itself to me in a most profound way because it is so very personal. Here is Mary Magdalene, who had already lost Jesus once; only just a few days before had she watched her beloved friend be horrifically executed—her friend, who had forgiven her and healed her and included her in his group of closest friends. And now his body, dead as it was, was gone, too.

I find it somewhat unsettling that Peter and John, some of Jesus' dearest friends, seem to have no emotional reaction to the fact that Jesus is missing from the tomb, no expression of sympathy or understanding for Mary's grief. John's record tells us only that they took a look around the tomb and then "went back to their homes." If there was any despairing between them, we don't know about it. By contrast, Mary's grief has just multiplied; her friend and teacher is not only dead, but his body has been unthinkably desecrated, dishonored by its removal to who knows where.

At our most desperate times, it can feel as if Jesus has been stolen from us, too. Grief, confusion, depression, anger, fear all conspire to convince us that God is nowhere near. For Mary, the disturbing presence of two mysterious figures in the tomb where Jesus' body should have been only added to the confusion and shock. She is like a tiny child who has gotten separated from her dad in a crowd, seeing only strangers when she should be seeing someone she loves.

Darkness

This sense of God's absence is mostly common, oddly enough, among those who have deep and mature faith. Many great saints have experienced the "dark night," a period when the sense of God's presence is unexplainably absent. Mother Teresa, known for her profound faith that expressed itself in service to "the poorest of the poor" had an experience of God's absence, revealed to the world only after her death. Likewise, the Son of God felt that his Father had abandoned him in his hour of deepest physical and spiritual pain.

We are told that Jesus will never leave us nor forsake us, but that doesn't mean we won't, at some point, feel that he has done exactly that. Scripture assures us that we can ascend to the heavens, make our bed in the depths, or "settle on the far side of the sea," but we cannot escape God's presence. That does not mean that we don't sometimes escape the *experience* of his presence.

At the tomb that day, Mary is not only despairing without Jesus, but she is abandoned by her friends when it was confirmed that Jesus' body was gone. In addition to the two strangers in the tomb, a third stranger arrives. Her tear-filled eyes fail her, but her reason does not: *it must be the gardener.*

Perhaps he will know what happened to the body, her Jesus, who is nowhere to be found.

Sometimes when we are in deep pain, our eyes can fail us, convincing us that Jesus has gone missing. Grief is a powerful force, and it can keep us from recognizing Jesus as he walks beside us on our own Emmaus road. The ability to see Jesus consistently and clearly is going to be tough as long as we're on this side of eternity (which is, of course, where faith comes in). I often think that it sure would be great if Jesus could just show up, in the flesh, so my ears could hear him say that everything is going to be okay, so I could see him and touch him and have every doubt erased. But I know that vision must wait for a future time. Paul, who experienced his own physical and spiritual blindness for a while, knew that kind of vision is not available to us while we walk about on earth. He explained it to his Corinthian friends: "For now we see in a mirror dimly, but then face to face. Now I know in part; then I shall know fully, even as I have been fully known" (1 Cor. 13:12 ESV).

Mary, as it turned out, would not have to wait that long. The "gardener" does indeed know where Jesus is, and he does something that instantly brings clear vision to her grief-stricken eyes. He says her name. "Mary." And she knows, even as she has been fully known, that it is Jesus. She experiences something of the great union with Jesus that all believers will one day know. This is what we have to look forward to: we will see him, healed and whole and standing before us. And he will call us by our name.

The Voice

Each of the Marys that we have considered knew Jesus well: Mary of Bethany was known as a friend of Jesus and listened to him speak; Mary, the mother of Jesus, probably knew his voice best of all, having tuned her ear to the voice of her son from the time of his first cry.

Mary Magdalene likewise knew Jesus' voice in ways that were particular to her experience. Mark 16:9 and Luke 8 tell of Mary Magdalene, "from whom he [Jesus] had cast out seven demons." Unlike the other two, this Mary of Magdala heard the voice of Jesus speak in power over evil forces that paralyzed her mind and soul, releasing her from their grip. Knowing, as we do, how Jesus managed similar situations elsewhere, he likely pronounced Mary forgiven, and then urged her to go and sin no more. These are the kinds of words Mary Magdalene heard from Jesus, and they would have been unforgettable.

Mary was not only freed *from* the evil grip of many demons, but freed *for* discipleship. Her healing completely changed her identity, allowing her to follow Jesus as one of his special friends, though the culture of the day would have frowned upon it. Her presence at the foot of the Cross, as well as caring for his broken body and attending to his tomb, is proof of her abiding loyalty to him. Jesus had spoken of himself as the Good Shepherd and said that his sheep know his voice; Mary Magdalene surely did.

Our familiarity with this story makes it difficult to fully appreciate what has just happened to Mary. Look again and see a woman whose understanding has just been shattered; the shock at finding Jesus' tomb empty, quickly followed by him standing before her fully alive, would have been tremendous. In just a few startling moments, Mary's understanding of Jesus is completely rearranged, magnified, expanded. Now she knows, by experience, that unlike everyone she had ever known, Jesus could not be defeated by death. Like Moses encountering the Lord in the burning bush, she couldn't possibly think about God in the same way again.

Mary and *Contemplatio*

Contemplatio, the final stage of *lectio divina*, leads us to deep peace and contentment in the loving presence of God. After listening and pondering and seeking God's direction, we can rest, assured of God's love for us. This is what Mary knew profoundly when Jesus said her name, assuring her that death had not won.

> Contemplative life is a human response to the fundamental fact that the central things in life, though spiritually perceptible, remain invisible in large measure and can very easily be overlooked by the inattentive, busy distracted person that each of us can so readily become. The contemplative looks not so much around things but through them into their center.[1]

Henri Nouwen wrote these words during an immersion experience into monastic life. By living, working, and praying alongside the Trappist monks at Genesee Abbey in New

York, he grew in his understanding of what contemplative life is about. He learned that contemplation isn't only a "stage" of prayerful reading, but it is a way of seeing and hearing all of life through God's eyes. All of life can become prayer when we learn to always be on the lookout for Jesus and when we attune our ears to the sound of his voice.

"The contemplation of God is not only the greatest honour to him, but the greatest profit to the soul."[2] Contemplation also leads us to an ever-expanding understanding of who God is. His capacity for love and ability to provide *shalom* reveal themselves as boundless; his authority in the universe staggers us. Our vision for the spiritual realm expands, teaching us to see in new and life-giving ways. Like Mary, we learn to say with ever-increasing confidence, "I have seen the Lord."

Mary Magdalene's response to Jesus demonstrates a contemplative posture as she becomes aware of spiritual realities that were initially invisible to her. As a result, she saw through the "center," as Nouwen suggests, even in the midst of her grief, and saw Jesus.

And Jesus saw her. It is one of the most beautiful moments in all of Scripture, a breathtaking image of what it means to love God and be loved by him. It is contemplation in its purest form—our desire for God is profoundly met when we find him in the deepest prayer of our heart, and simultaneously we are found by him and receive his sacrificial love for us. "[M]editation and contemplative prayer, is not so much a way to find God as a way of resting in him whom we have *found*, who loves us, who is near to us, who comes to us to draw us to himself."[3] There is nothing greater in the human experience than knowing, experientially, that we are deeply loved by God.

This deep, experiential knowing of the love of God empowers Mary to do what Jesus asks her to do: "Go to my brothers and say to them, 'I am ascending to my Father and your Father, to my God and your God.'" When we are given the vision of the fierce love of God for us, we are empowered to enter the world more fully as his agents of redemption, his kingdom ambassadors. Without such an awareness of his love, we are left to our own shallow store of resources that is quickly depleted.

To contemplate the truth of the risen Christ and his love is the exact opposite of distraction. It's where we must fix our gaze. And there is no sweeter vision.

Notes

[1] Henri Nouwen, *The Genesee Diary* (New York: Image, 1981), 36–37.

[2] Robert Llewelyn, *With Pity Not with Blame: Contemplative Praying with Julian of Norwich & the Cloud of Unknowing* (Norwich, UK: Canterbury Press, 2013), 11.

[3] Thomas Merton, *Contemplative Prayer* (New York: Image, 1996), 29.

chapter 12

contemplatio for life

There is nothing like looking, if you want to find something. . . .
You certainly usually find something, if you look, but it is not
always quite the something you were after.[1]

Easter arrived smack in the middle of Cary's sabbatical leave last spring, the halfway point of our six-week residence in England's Peak District. I remember planning our itinerary in the months prior and thinking it fortuitous that we'd be in England for Easter. I imagined us in a grand Anglican cathedral somewhere with all the bells and smells that the highest of holy days called for. Instead, we found ourselves in a tiny Methodist church with no more than thirty others. We had attended the church a time or two already, and in the end, we decided that we'd like to celebrate Easter with faces that were at least somewhat familiar. It was a good decision.

In the early part of the service, the minister asked if the children of the church would like to come up front and share their "Easter gardens" with us. Three small girls came forward, each carrying a clear plastic tray filled with dark soil, moss, twigs, and rocks—their Sunday school project of the day. The minister then asked the oldest to describe her garden, and she obediently pointed out the pathway of pebbles and the cross of twigs and the mound of stones that was the tomb. I thought it extremely clever.

The minister then leaned closer to the tiniest of girls, who couldn't have been more than three and, pointing to the empty tomb, asked (in his very proper British accent), "And what have we got in there?"

"A troll," said the little girl, matter-of-factly (to my ears it sounded like "trOH-wel"). The minister didn't seem to understand her at all, so he asked her again. Her response was the same: "A TROLL." It was then all we could do to stifle our giggles; the little girl was obviously imagining an altogether different story than the one we were celebrating that day.

Or maybe, like Mary, she simply wasn't seeing clearly. A troll, a gardener—either way, Jesus was not seen. Not at first, anyway.

Contemplatio for Life

When practicing *lectio divina* with Scripture, we are given three different exposures to that Scripture before arriving at the fourth—*contemplatio*—which is meant to lead us into a resting assurance of the presence and love of God. That rest is available to us because we have been led to it via the repeated meditation on the passage. By the time we've read it three times, ruminating on it and asking God to lead us to a response, we are convinced of the reality of his living, loving presence with us. We know with certainty that he inhabits his Word and meets us there.

In the same way, pondering what is before us in *life*—ruminating, responding—we learn to recognize Christ's presence before us in ways we've not been able to do before. Where once we saw everything *but* Jesus—busyness, obstacles, stress, anxiety (perhaps even trolls?)—now his presence is unmistakable. Our meditative posture has made us more alert to the tracks of Jesus, to the fingerprints he leaves behind. We begin to recognize the work he is doing; we discern the breeze of the Holy Spirit. *We hear him say our name.* And we are convinced, once and for all, that there is nothing more that we could possibly need. He is the end and the joy of all our desiring.

Mary of Magdalene's experience in the tomb mirrors the stages of *lectio divina*: she looked for him, she pondered the troubling mystery of his body being gone, she asked for help, and finally she came to know, even as she is fully known: "Mary." Her search was over, her longing was made complete. This is the objective of the pondering process. Distractions no longer keep us from Jesus. Instead, they are overcome and replaced with the realization of his presence.

Kindred Spirits

I am forever looking for others who can teach me about longing for Jesus and finding him, seeing him. The search can be frustrating, given that we live in an environment that is more conducive to shallow faith versus one of depth and substance. Often, I have turned to the past, to kindred spirits who lived exemplary lives of deep passion for Christ. Their writings teach and correct me when I am tempted to live only on the surface of things. They are voices from another time, and they faced different kinds of distractions, yet their wisdom transcends the time gap between us. They serve as mentors, as spiritual directors, coaxing me forward into deep communion with Jesus. They have names like Lewis and Nouwen, Patrick and Teresa, à Kempis and Kelley.

> For this is the reason why we are not fully at ease in heart and soul: because here we seek rest in these things that are so little, in which there is no rest and we recognize not our God who is all powerful, all wise, all good, for He is the true rest.[2]

These are the words of Lady Julian of Norwich, England, who lived in the fourteenth century as an anchoress—a woman of solitary prayer—in a small stone cell attached to a church. Such a life makes little sense to our modern sensibilities, which, on the face of it, makes Julian an unlikely candidate for a spiritual guide. Unless, of course, we believe that the prayer and spiritual counsel Julian offered actually play an integral role in God's work in and intentions for the world.

In Julian's time, her work was indeed seen as critical, and she was honored for choosing such a life. Her small cell included three windows: one that linked her to the church, so she could receive the Eucharist; one that was accessed by attendants who brought her food and necessities; and one that opened to the world, where she would receive visitors coming for spiritual support and guidance. So it cannot be said that Julian's choice was a selfish one. Rather, she shows us a way in which a deep love for God results in a deep love for people.

Her book, *Revelations of Divine Love*, is the first book written in English by a woman. It details a series of visions granted to her, out of which Julian received new understanding of Christ's love for her and for the world. Her contemplative wisdom is hailed by such noted figures as T. S. Eliot and Dallas Willard, and Thomas Merton believed her to be "without doubt one of the most wonderful of all Christian voices."[3]

Julian is famously credited with the words, "All shall be well, and all shall be well, and all manner of thing shall be well." One can see why it is so frequently quoted; we all need as much encouragement we can get, and hearing that everything will be okay is sometimes all the guidance I need. But the quotation is rarely cited in its complete form. The full citation is even better. For the words are not

Julian's; they are Christ's words to Julian, and she describes the exchange in her book:

> And because of the tender love that our good
> Lord has to all that shall be saved, He comforts
> quickly and sweetly, meaning thus: 'It is true that
> sin is cause of all this pain,
>> but all shall be well,
>> and all shall be well,
>> and all manner of thing shall be well.'
> These words were said most tenderly, showing no
> manner of blame to me nor to any that shall be
> saved.[4]

This is not a flippant expression of wishful thinking. But Jesus himself will make all things well, even in the face of sin. The famous saying is not empty sentimentalism but a declaration of Christ's love for us that goes beyond our earthly circumstances.

I think it is not unreasonable to think that this is the kind of love Christ showed to Mary, reassuring her that even death had been conquered, that he was alive indeed. Is it assuming too much to think that Jesus says these words—in love—to us as well? Isn't it logical to conclude that the one who said, "I am making all things new" (Rev. 21:5 ESV) is likewise assuring us that in the fullness of time, all will indeed be well?

Through her many years in her cell—forty, perhaps—Julian gained a tremendous capacity for God's love. And while it came to her through much suffering, she believed the merciful love of Christ is accessible to all who will receive it. "It is God's will that we have true delight with Him in our salvation and in that He wishes us to be mightily comforted and strengthened, and thus He wills that with His grace our soul can be happily engaged, for we are His bliss, for in us He delights without end and so shall we in Him with His grace."[5]

Yearning for God

When we detect God's love in our daily lives, drink it in, and soak it up, we will begin to grasp the deeper things of God and know the fullness with which he dearly loves the world. Christians are known, Jesus said, by their love. But it is not just any kind of love. It is qualitatively different than the love that the rest of the world knows. This love is demonstrated in actions, yes, but also in *presence*, alerting the world to the reality of Jesus in us. The more we receive the love of Jesus, the more we can *be* the love of Jesus.

The anonymous writer of *The Cloud of Unknowing* claimed that "one loving blind desire for God alone is . . . more helpful to your friends . . . than anything else you could do."[6] Can this be true? Those who position themselves as enemies of God will argue that violence and atrocities have been committed in abundance in the name of God. What cannot be disputed, however, is that great movements of healing, of justice, of humanitarian relief, of civil rights have been accomplished by people of faith—not only because they were people of principle, but because they were channels of the love of God. There is real divine stuff at work here.

And there are infinite possibilities of further works of reform and healing for those whose desire for God and his love is a driving force. "Flee to our Lord and we shall be comforted," Julian says. "Touch him and we shall be made clean. Cling to him and we shall be safe and sound from every kind of danger. For our courteous Lord wills that we should be as at home with him as heart may think or soul may desire."[7]

God Is Enough

Julian's era was marked by a series of events and conditions that would challenge the faith of the strongest among us. She survived three waves of the Black Plague that wiped out half the population of East Anglia, saw both king and archbishop assassinated, witnessed the widespread rioting of the Peasants' Rebellion, and saw the beginning of the Hundred Years' War between England and France.[8] She sustained life-threatening illnesses of her own, the most noted of which corresponded with the "revelations of divine love" she received from the Lord and subsequently wrote about. Julian emerged from her suffering with a single-eyed focus:

> God, of Thy goodness, give me Thyself;
> For Thou art enough to me,
> And I can ask nothing that is less
> That can be full honor to Thee.

And if I ask anything that is less,
Ever shall I be in want,
For only in Thee have I all.[9]

As Julian yearned for God, she grew ever aware of his yearning for us, speaking of his people as "God's special friends," and of him as our "everlasting friend." The Four Marys seem to have had this kind of relationship with Jesus, especially Mary of Bethany and Mary Magdalene. Scripture tells us that Lazarus was considered Jesus' friend. Peter, James, and John were known to have an especially close relationship with Jesus. So, yes, Jesus knew true friendship on earth. We should take care, however, lest we adopt a cavalier attitude with regard to our own friendship with Jesus; he is not something precious we keep in our pocket. He is indeed a king, but a king who condescends to make a slave a friend.

Giving and Receiving

Long ago, my spiritual director taught me a simple pattern of prayer for the purpose of drawing me more deeply into the love of God. Margaret called it "the love exchange,"[10] and it is one of the most meaningful spiritual practices I've encountered. Through it we can begin to grasp the truth that Julian knew: we not only need to grow in our ability to love God, but we are also greatly impaired in our ability to receive God's love for us in a way that is real and transforming.

There are many reasons for this inability to believe in the scope of God's love for us, one being the distractions that we've already labeled as a major enemy. Other obstacles loom large: the belief that we are unlovable, or undeserving of God's love because of our innate and ongoing sinfulness; the ways we've been mistreated by authorities in our lives, making it nearly impossible to believe in a loving God; the lack of integrity found too often in the church, causing us to question the reality of a God who loves unconditionally. The reasons go on, each tethered to human experiences that reside in our storehouse of memories.

What the love exchange does is put us in a place where we can receive God's love by faith, the nature of which requires us to step out and believe even when we can't see proof before our eyes. God loved us first, and so the first step in the love exchange is to ponder scriptural passages that declare his love for us.[11] Whether we *feel* that love or not is no matter. As we review the scriptural declarations of God's love, we receive his love *by faith*, trusting that God's Word is true. "So we have come to know and to believe the love that God has for us. God is love, and whoever abides in love abides in God, and God abides in him" (1 John 4:16 ESV).

Next, in response, we speak (silently or audibly) our love to God in return. This is when we may discover how small our love for God actually is, but we give it all to him nonetheless. We respond to him, with the help of the Holy Spirit, with all the love we have.

The whole process may last only a few minutes.

When is the last time you came to prayer only for the purpose of receiving God's love and loving him in return? What might happen in your life if this became a regular pattern, a daily exposure to the life-giving love of God?

The pattern described here is one that can be part of a daily time with God. However, experience tells me that this same pattern can be appropriated in the midst of real life with traffic and laundry and email. Instead of receiving God's love via the printed word, we can watch for his expressions of love that come to us in many ordinary ways.

Spiritual Myopia

Fr. John-Julian, author of *The Complete Julian of Norwich*, says,

> God surrounds and encloses us—and most of the time we do not know it because we are not looking or seeing the Divine Reality on whom we are grounded. There has been no wrathful withdrawing on God's part; there is only sinful myopia on our parts. God is not dead and not "gone" for Julian; for her God is utterly present in our nature and soul, but often invisible because of our own inadequate sight.[12]

Many are the messages of love that are sent to us each day, yet they go unnoticed and without response from us. It doesn't have to be this way. "Always be in a state of expectancy," says Oswald Chambers, "and see that you leave room for God to come in as He likes."[13]

We have been going through a difficult period with Rory, our goldendoodle puppy. For some unknown reason, she's become wakeful in the night, whining at least once in the early hours of the morning to tell us she needs to go out. This is merely an annoyance, certainly not in the category of real problems. Yet annoying it is. We thought our days of getting up with the baby were long behind us.

Now and then, I will let Cary sleep, and I will do dog duty in the middle of the night. I'm a light sleeper, so I become alert rather quickly. I've noticed that those middle-of-the-night forays into the darkness have become oddly rewarding. For when the night is clear and the weather is still, there is a beauty that is missed when I'm blissfully asleep. The stars are spectacular; I hear an owl's mournful hooting; the rustling of the trees tells me the deer are nearby; the full moon creates shadows like the midafternoon sun. And for those few moments, there is the whisper of love from God to a woman in her pajamas and her rascal of a dog. It makes returning to my warm bed even more gratifying. I whisper some love back to God as I drift off, a simple exchange in unremarkable circumstances.

Evidence

If the heavens can declare the glory of God (Ps. 19:1 esv), then human beings, who have voices and hands and bear his own image, can do the job even better. When we have ears to hear, the love messages of God are quite easy to discern as they are transmitted—wittingly or unwittingly—from person to person.

Today I listened to a young colleague tell me of her experiences leading a recovery group for teenaged girls. She told me some of their hard stories of abuse, addiction, self-harming. The way they support each other in those dark places is beautiful, evidence of the redemptive work of God. But as she spoke, it was my friend's tears that betrayed God's love in her, love planted deeply in her heart and growing and bearing fruit for young ones who may not yet have ears to hear.

> O the deep, deep love of Jesus, vast, unmeasured,
>   boundless, free!
> Rolling as a mighty ocean in its fullness over me!
> Underneath me, all around me, is the current of
>   Thy love
> Leading onward, leading homeward to Thy glorious
>   rest above![14]

I think of Mary of Magdalene—contemplative, heartsick Mary—whose despair is instantly erased at the sight of her Jesus. The words of this great hymn provide the perfect soundtrack, the ideal accompaniment for what happened at that moment of recognition, of reunion. The deep, deep love of Jesus is what she longed for, and likewise what Julian of Norwich yearned for more than anything.

"One thing I ask from the LORD," says the psalmist, "this only do I seek: that I may dwell in the house of the

LORD all the days of my life, to gaze on the beauty of the LORD and to seek him in his temple" (Ps. 27:4). Like Mary Magdalene, Julian knew *contemplatio*—rest in the presence and love of God.

Prayer

O God, the Father of all humankind,

you bid us listen to your son, the well-beloved.

Nourish our hearts on your word,

purify the eyes of our mind,

and fill us with joy at the vision of your glory.

We ask this through our Lord Jesus Christ your Son,

who lives and reigns with you and the Holy Spirit,

one God forever and ever.[15]

Amen.

Notes

[1] J. R. R. Tolkien, *The Annotated Hobbit* (New York: HarperCollins, 2003), 105.

[2] John-Julian, CMS 14.72, 14.74, *The Complete Julian of Norwich* (Brewster, MA: Paraclete, 2009), 79.

[3] Ibid., 3.

[4] Ibid., 149.

[5] Ibid., 137.

[6] *The Cloud of Unknowing*, ed. William Johnston (New York: Image, 1973), 60.

[7] Robert Llewelyn, *With Pity Not with Blame: Contemplative Praying with Julian of Norwich & The Cloud of Unknowing* (Norwich, UK: Canterbury Press, 2013), 17–18.

[8] John-Julian, *Complete Julian*, 5.

[9] Ibid., 79.

[10] Margaret Therkelsen, *The Love Exchange: An Adventure in Prayer* (Lexington, KY: Bristol Books, 1990).

[11] Scripture passages that declare God's love for us, as cited in Margaret Therkelsen, *The Love Exchange*: Proverbs 8:17; Isaiah 30:18; Isaiah 41:9; Isaiah 43:1–2, 4, 25; Isaiah 45:2–3; Isaiah 46:4; Isaiah 54:5, 10, 17; Jeremiah 31:3; Zephaniah 3:17; John 3:16; John 14:21, 23; John 15:9; Ephesians 2:4–7; 1 John 3:1–2; 1 John 4:16, 19.

[12] John-Julian, *Complete Julian*, 11.

[13] David McCasland, ed., *The Quotable Oswald Chambers* (Grand Rapids, MI: Discovery House, 2008).

[14] "O the Deep, Deep Love of Jesus," lyrics by Samuel Trevor Francis, music by Thomas J. Williams, © Copyright 1931. Renewed 1959 Nazarene Publishing House (admin. by the Copyright Company, Nashville, TN). All rights reserved. Used by permission.

[15] The Community of Jesus, *The Little Book of Hours: Praying with the Community of Jesus* (Brewster, MA: Paraclete, 2003), 143.

recognition

Journal
May 6, 2014
Julian's Cell, St. Julian's Church
Norwich, England

"I am he who makes you to love. I am he who makes you to long. I am he the endless fulfilling of all true desires."[1]

Here in Julian's cell, adjoined to St Julian's church, it is serene and small, but not suffocating. There is a high ceiling, a large altar with a white altar cloth, and a large—*very* large—stone crucifix hanging on the wall behind it.

I was just part of a small group that gathered here for an afternoon meditation, led by a woman named Denise. There were about ten of us, and we fit perfectly on the bench that stretches along two sides of the cell walls. Denise is warm and soft-spoken and smiles constantly as she talks. Her meditation seemed quite true to Julian, from what I'm learning, with a strong emphasis on God's love for us. In talking with her afterward, I gather that our understanding of theology differs, but no matter. Her former Buddhism led her back to the church, and she is listening to God now, with the aid of Julian. She and I just discovered a delightful "coincidence": she is going to be on Iona all next week with her Celtic harpist friend—the very week my pilgrim group and I will be there. Yes, we will find her, and yes, we'll be thrilled to hear her friend play the harp on Iona. I love it when God reveals connections like this. They happen with uncanny frequency.

The more I read Julian, and the more I learn about her via these people and this place, the more I sense that she is for me. She was a woman of prayer, of contemplation, filled with love for God. A woman of vision, confident of God's messages of love for her. I'm so grateful to be here at the very spot where she lived and prayed and received friends who needed her counsel.

I light three prayer candles and pray for the eyes of my heart to be open.

May 7, 2014
Julian's Cell, St. Julian's Church
Norwich, England

It is quite remarkable to be sitting here again, in the same place (now restored) where Julian received her "showings," almost to the day, May 8, nearly seven hundred years ago.

Today I revisit John 20, especially as Jesus' words to Julian are my center: "Lo, how I have loved you." My favorite and familiar story of Mary at the tomb always reveals new truth, no matter how many times I return to it.

I am pondering the transmissions of love from Jesus to Mary. First, his recognition that she is upset. (The angels have also shown this concern. It's worth noting that their question to her was not, "What are you doing here?" but "Woman, why are you crying?") And Mary was completely distraught, grieving the loss of her teacher and friend, despairing that she cannot express her love by reverently caring for his broken body.

She has not recognized him by sight . . . but when he says her name, she knows. "My sheep recognize my voice." And he clearly knows her. There is love that is exchanged when we truly know one another, when we truly know Christ.

What I don't understand is why, after reading this so many times before, do I only now see that nowhere in the text does it say she fell at his feet and held on? This is always how I've imagined the scene, and while it may very well have been that way, the text does not specify it. We only read that Jesus had to ask her not to hold on. I think this gives permission to imagine a full embrace: "Lo, how I have loved you." Jesus did not shoo her away, but loved her deeply before he told her what she must now do. And it was out of the reality of that loving embrace that Mary had the ability to go and tell as her Lord requested.

What would it be like if I lived each moment in the knowledge of Jesus' embracing love? If I didn't simply live with the knowledge of Christ sitting beside me, but Christ hugging me to himself? If I thought of Christ's love as more than something that "travels" to me, but that is always as near to me as if he were hugging me in the flesh?

How can I live daily in the reality of Jesus' embrace?

May 8, 2014
Train
Norwich to Sheffield

I did not sleep well last night. I went to bed earlier than usual, which may have been part of the problem. And I fussed because the pillow in my guesthouse room smelled funny to me. Me and my nose . . . smelling is my superpower, say my children. The result of it all was that I ended up sleeping a bit longer this morning than planned.

My first stop this morning was at the Julian Centre gift shop, immediately next door to the guesthouse, where I picked up three Julian icons, one for myself, and one for Kim and Lisa each. Then I returned to Julian's cell yet again to spend some time. I was the only one there for the entire hour or so, which was nice, but it was still rather noisy; various deliveries were being made and set-ups had to be managed for the annual Julian Week celebration. My hostess, Sister Pamela—the sole proprietor of the guest house—made me chuckle as she scrambled around the church and gardens, nervously waiting for the marquis (tent) to arrive and be set up to accommodate some of the events. Never mind that she also would be cooking for guests, including the former Archbishop of Canterbury, Rowan Williams. I would have loved to have been present at that table!

A Julian-themed lecture was scheduled for just after noon at the library in the middle of the city, so I set off walking to arrive in time. There is loads of tempting shopping in Norwich, including a huge open market. I resisted it successfully, knowing I'd be frustrated with myself if I traded the lecture for some indiscriminate browsing.

The theme of the lecture, given by an Anglican priest, was the role of pain and suffering in our lives, for Julian had endured many painful trials of her own. I've never believed that pain and suffering were something that God was okay with; I believe all of the rotten effects of the fall displease him greatly, and that he suffers with us in our pain and seeks to bring redemption in the midst of it. Today's lecture reminded me that suffering is sometimes needed in this broken world in order to purify us, to stretch and grow us, to give us a clearer vision in which God becomes central and the self fades.

I will never believe that God brings tornadoes for our good, or that a car accident that wipes out an entire family is his plan, or that there is a "reason" a rogue shooter in an elementary school is part of God's grand design; he simply cannot be the author of evil. But Julian's writings make me willing to think more about the way pain is used by God. I teach my university students about God's ability to redeem even the worst events and conditions in our world. But today our lecturer helped me see that what is essential in that process is reflection. That when pain and suffering are accompanied by prayerful reflection—reflection that is rooted in a confident understanding of the love of God— then *wisdom* is the result. He said that presence or absence of reflection is what makes the difference between one who is bitter and broken because of pain, and one who emerges wiser and stronger. I will be thinking about this a good long while.

Also, something very strange happened during the lecture.

I was sitting on the end of a row of chairs, up against a temporary wall that had been set up to separate our group from the rest of the library where the Julian sessions were held this week. Two of these sections of temporary wall came together to make a sort of corner right next to me, leaving a small amount of space between them. On the other side of the wall from where I sat, stood a man, who worked himself into that corner space as best he could, apparently in order to listen to the lecture.

The way he was dressed made me nervous—quite grungy—and there was something about his behavior that made me uneasy. (Why didn't he just come in with the rest of us and take a seat? Why was he sort of half in, half out?) And then my hypersensitive nose kicked in again and picked up a smell—not foul, exactly, but definitely dirty. I really, really wanted him to leave, though I struggled internally about it. It wasn't his appearance or even his smell that made me twitchy. The fact that he was there but not there just bothered me. Yet there he stood, the entire time, even appearing to listen at times.

At the end of the talk, our lecturer invited questions, and someone promptly offered a very good one, though I don't remember what it was. As soon as it was sufficiently answered by the lecturer, Grungy Standing Man on the other side of my wall began speaking loudly, and in his very strong cockney accent made a clear and impassioned statement that JESUS AND HIS LOVE MUST BE AT THE CENTER OF ALL OF OUR CONVERSATIONS ABOUT JULIAN. He sounded a little drunk and definitely fit the part of the crazy guy, but he was actually making a good bit of sense. If someone would have transcribed what he said, I feel quite sure it would read very coherently. Our lecturer handled the somewhat awkward disruption very graciously. And fortunately, the man stopped just short of an all-out rant. But surprisingly, I detected a voice or two from the crowd expressing support for what he was saying. I might have been one of them.

Grungy-but-Wise Man left, unprompted, after his unsolicited speech. And somehow the crowd, thirty or more of us, seemed to absorb what was positive about it and let anything negative roll right off. The questions and discussion that followed were very good and helpful. I wondered whether it was an unstable man or a heavenly messenger who had just been with us.

I think if Julian had been sitting there with us, she would have known the answer to that query. After all of those years of silent listening to God's voice, she would have recognized God's voice in this man if it was there, and likewise, she would immediately know if the voice was not of God at all.

Those are the ears I want, that is the heart I want—a heart that responds with love in the presence of its truest Love.

Note

[1] Robert Llewelyn, *With Pity Not with Blame: Contemplative Praying with Julian of Norwich & The Cloud of Unknowing* (Norwich, UK: Canterbury Press, 2013), 53.

chapter 14

active contemplation

Our life and how we find the world now and in the future is, almost totally, a simple result of what we have become in the depths of our being—in our spirit, will, or heart. From there we see our world and interpret reality. From there we make our choices, break forth into action, try to change our world. We live from our depths—most of which we do not understand.

—Dallas Willard[1]

We've been on a journey together, exploring what it means to move from superficial faith to deeply rooted faith, from distraction to focus, from the shallows to the depths. It's a journey that will, I hope, force us out of the mind-set of easy-access, drive-through spirituality and leave us standing with our jaws hanging open just a bit, grateful that we have eternity to continue experiencing life with our unfathomable God.

We've learned from the Four Marys that when life is lived in the depths with God, qualities like stillness, humility, reverence, and clarity will emerge. We've seen them admirably demonstrate the ability to listen to God, ponder his Word and ways, respond in adoration, and contemplate his love. It's been a lot to take in. It leaves us with a question that has yet to be answered fully: Is there any real practical purpose for contemplation, beyond what it does for me?

This entire discussion has been intentionally directed inward, true enough. Our formation into Christlikeness has to begin with the formation of our individual souls. Yet all of that can sound a bit self-centered; the last thing this world needs is more people who are fixated on themselves. So what *does* the world need? Is there any chance that the world actually needs contemplatives? My answer to that rhetorical question is, of course, yes. Lest we think that all of this internal work is only for our own good, let's consider three compelling reasons for the presence of contemplatives in the world.

Contemplation informs action.

"A contemplative . . . makes the love of God his main, his only object in life."[2] The easy assumption about a life that is characterized by things like silence, meditation, and contemplation is that such a person is of little use in a world where things need to get done. And we're not just talking about tasks that need doing, but about the real and selfless kinds of work that are required in a world that hurts as ours does.

If the love of God is the contemplative's primary focus in life, then sacrificial love and service will be the result. The image of Mother Teresa immediately comes to mind. While she was known throughout the world for her commitment to the poorest of the poor, she would be grieved to think that was the complete definition of her life's work. Love was always her aim; love was her fuel. The love of God compelled her as an active contemplative. "Ask yourself 'How has [Jesus] loved me? Do I really love others in the same way?' Unless this love is among us, we can kill ourselves with work and it will only be work, not love. Work without love is slavery."[3] Contemplation leads to love in action.

Contemplation brings wholeness to a world that is dis-integrating.

> When I have learned to read God's word in the book of my everyday life, then I am aware of a continuity and wholeness integrating all that I do in the course of the day . . . not only my sacred reading (*lectio divina*) but my work . . . my interaction with others, my appreciation of nature, music, art—everything may become a medium through which the Word speaks to me.[4]

The contemplative lives out of the unifying principle that the love of God and his Word weave in and out of our everyday lives in transforming, healing ways. But few in the world are actually aware of this miraculous presence.

> Why are we able to master great technology, but do not yet understand our own hearts. Why, after

centuries, are we still so far from understanding the nature of love? And why are we willing to make endless outer journeys, but are loath to make the significant one: the journey within. The inward journey may frighten us, yet it is this journey which holds the real treasure. There God's spirit waits to reveal mysteries and beauty beyond our imagination: the secrets of what is holy, and the encounters with truth that change everything.[5]

The world is a mass of confusion. The contemplative can bring some order and meaning to the table. Not by providing answers, but by a thoughtful model of deeply rooted peace and purpose.

Contemplation turns us into love.

Christians are called to love, to be vessels of Christ's love to the world. Contemplation takes us one step closer: the more we love God and receive his love in return, the more we become his love. Love does not just move in and out and through us, but in a very real sense we are becoming love. This is what happens to people who determine to follow Christ and be changed into his image. "We begin to see all of life's experiences as ways for learning to love with his love. We soon recognize that the only true mark of Jesus is his free-flowing love in our lives."[6]

This is important not only for our witness and service to the world, but to our fellow Christians. We in the church need to remind each other that Jesus said everyone will know we belong to him by the way we love each other. That love needs to be nurtured and tended carefully. Sadly, many believers are no longer affiliated with a local congregation because of painful experiences there. I sometimes ask my college students how many in the room have experienced a split in their church; nearly fifty percent of the class raises their hands, to my great sadness. I read about the fallout of these experiences in the papers I ask them to write, and it's distressing. The lack of love for each other has come to characterize too many of the worship centers in our country.

I was in Landshut, Germany, this year for Pentecost Sunday. Along with Tim, our colleague and friend, Cary and I led a group of university students in a four-week study abroad experience. Pentecost Sunday found us worshipping with the local Catholic community in magnificent St. Martin's basilica.

The entire service was in German, of course, so we were limited in our ability to participate in recalling the arrival of the Holy Spirit in Acts 2. That is, until they began falling—hundreds, thousands of rose petals, red, pink, blush, from the ceiling. And in the midst of this steady stream of floating petals was a silver-cast dove, held by a thin tether, coming down from the same ceiling until it hovered above seven candles and the priest who was lighting them.

Little children were allowed to walk up the aisle and gather handfuls of the fragrant petals. The towering arches of the church, the great crucifix—more than 25 feet high—and

the massive building filled with worshipers did not intim-
idate them; they ran back and forth, picking up petals and
delivering them to loved ones in the pews.

This is what happens when we respond to the invitation
from God. He comes down to us, we open our hands to
receive him, and then we take and give him to others. And
it is beautiful.

Coming Full Circle

We began this venture with an invitation:

> Come, all you who are thirsty,
> > come to the waters;
> and you who have no money,
> > come, buy and eat!
> Come, buy wine and milk
> > without money and without cost.
> Why spend money on what is not bread,
> > and your labor on what does not satisfy?
> Listen, listen to me, and eat what is good,
> > and you will delight in the richest of fare.
> Give ear and come to me;
> > listen, that you may live.
> (Isa. 55:1-3)

As we bring it to a close by examining the purpose and
usefulness of contemplation—of why God does indeed give
us permission to ponder—the remaining verses of Isaiah's
chapter contribute to the conversation:

> Seek the LORD while he may be found;
> call on him while he is near. . . .
> You will go out in joy
> and be led forth in peace;
> the mountains and hills
> will burst into song before you,
> and all the trees of the field
> will clap their hands.
> Instead of the thornbush will grow the juniper,
> and instead of briers the myrtle will grow.
> This will be for the LORD's renown,
> for an everlasting sign,
> that will endure forever.
>
> (Isa. 55:6, 12–13)

Those who give ear to the Lord will be vessels of joy, peace . . . and healing. People who embody the deep, deep love of Jesus serve as agents of redemption, cultivating juniper and myrtle where thorns and briers once ruled. And it will not be for a moment, or a season. It will be forever, an everlasting tribute to the Lord.

You and I have been given permission to ponder, because the world needs people who are deeply connected to the love of God. "For I tell you this, one loving blind desire for God alone is . . . more helpful to your friends . . . than anything else you could do."[7]

Notes

[1] Dallas Willard, *Renovation of the Heart* (Colorado Springs, CO: NavPress, 2002), 13.

[2] A. H. N. Green-Armytage, quoted in Richard Foster, *Streams of Living Water: Celebrating the Great Traditions of Christian Faith* (New York: HarperCollins, 1998), 33.

[3] Mother Teresa, *Come Be My Light* (New York: Image, 2007).

[4] Charles Cummings, *Monastic Practices* (Kalamazoo, MI: Cistercian, 1986), 20.

[5] Paula D'Arcy, *Gift of the Red Bird: A Spiritual Encounter* (New York: Crossroad, 1996), 14.

[6] Margaret Therkelsen, *The Love Exchange: An Adventure in Prayer* (Lexington, KY: Bristol Books, 1990), 42.

[7] William Johnston, ed., *The Cloud of Unknowing* (New York: Image, 1973), 60.

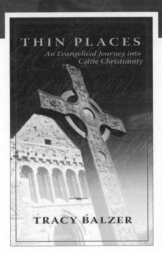

Having trouble finding class and small group material?

Check out our free class and small group resource guide. Inside you will find books from ACU Press & Leafwood Publishers that your members can use to facilitate or lead, no matter their level of experience. All of these books include study and discussion questions.

CLASS & SMALL GROUP RESOURCE GUIDE
SUMMER 2015

Abilene Christian University Press

LEAFWOOD
P U B L I S H E R S

Ask about our bulk discounts for churches.

877-816-4455 (toll free)
www.acupressbooks.com
www.leafwoodpublishers.com.

~ Book descriptions
~ Sorted by categories:

* Prayer
* Women
* Textual Studies
* and Many More!

Be sure to check back with us as we continue to add more resources.

Abilene Christian University Press

LEAFWOOD
P U B L I S H E R S